MW01670576

Copyright© 2018 by Your Quirky Aunt
ALL RIGHTS RESERVED. By purchase of this book, you have been licensed one copy for personal use only. No part of this work may be reproduced, redistributed, or used in any form or by any means without prior written permission of the publisher and copyright owner.

Your Quirky Aunt

Calling All Wine Lovers!

Your Quirky Aunt would like to thank you for taking the time to buy and color my book!
As a thank you I want you to enter our Personalized Wine Glass Set Giveaway!

Personalized Wine Glass Set includes:

Set of wine glasses with your choice of monogram, design, or artwork!

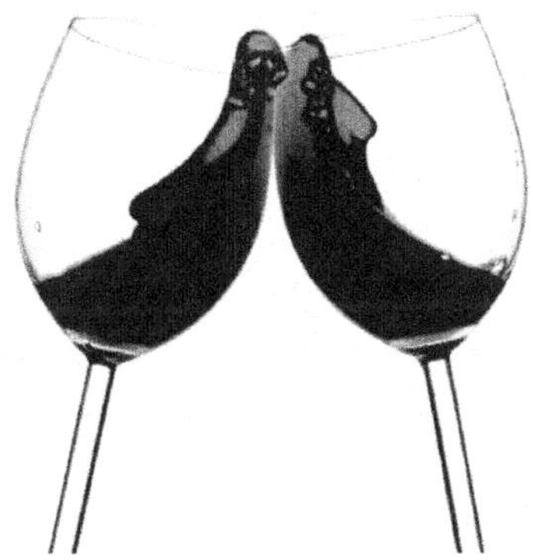

All you have to do is email us with your feedback about our new On Cloud Wine - Adult Coloring Book! We will select an entry Every other month for this set! .

Email us for a chance to wine our monthly

** PERSONALIZED WINE GLASS SET**

YOURQUIRKYAUNT@GMAIL.COM

If you enjoy our products, please leave us a review on Amazon to help support our small business!

Stay Awesome!

Your Quirky Aunt

Follow Us on Facebook:
Your Quirky Aunt

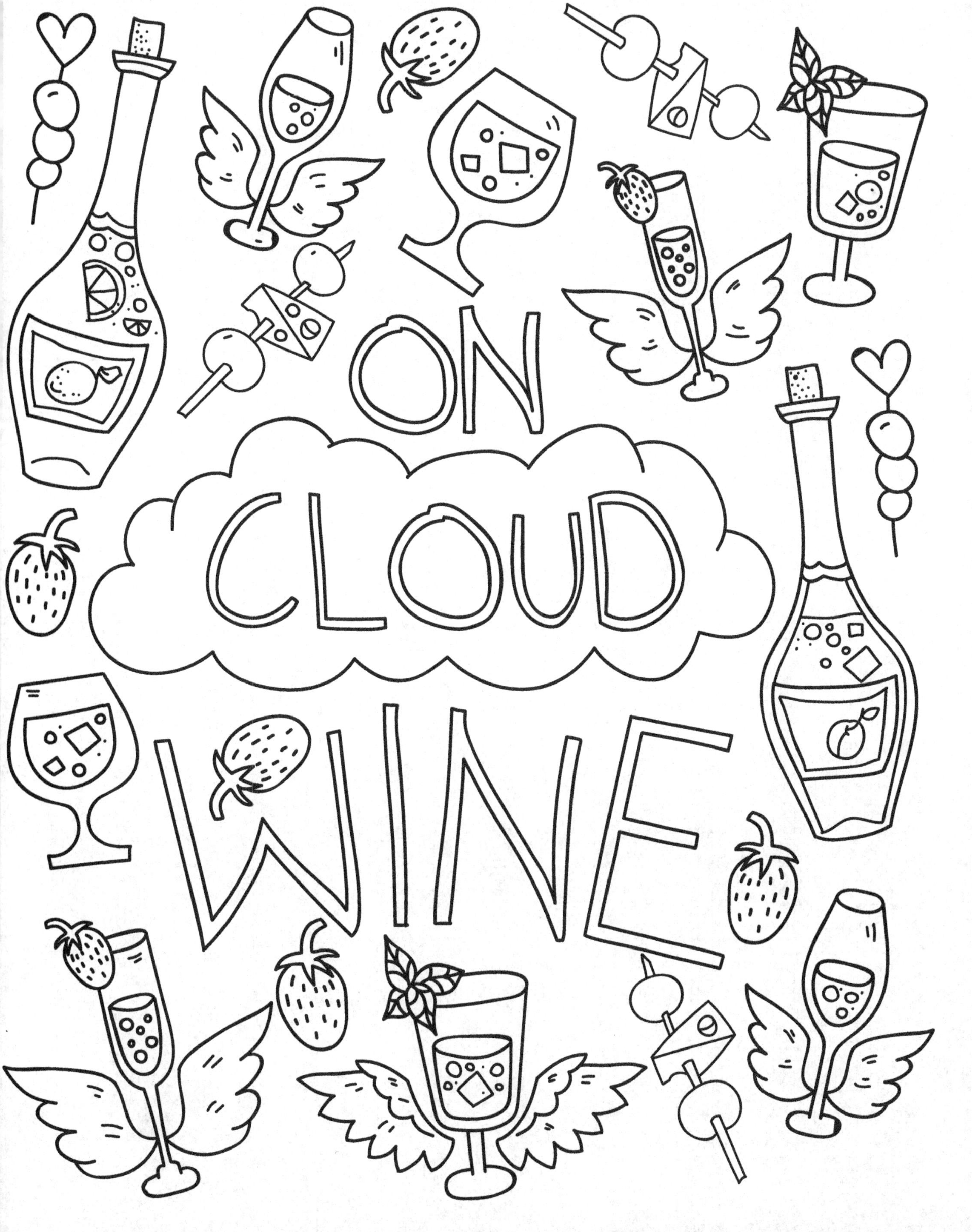
ON
CLOUD
WINE

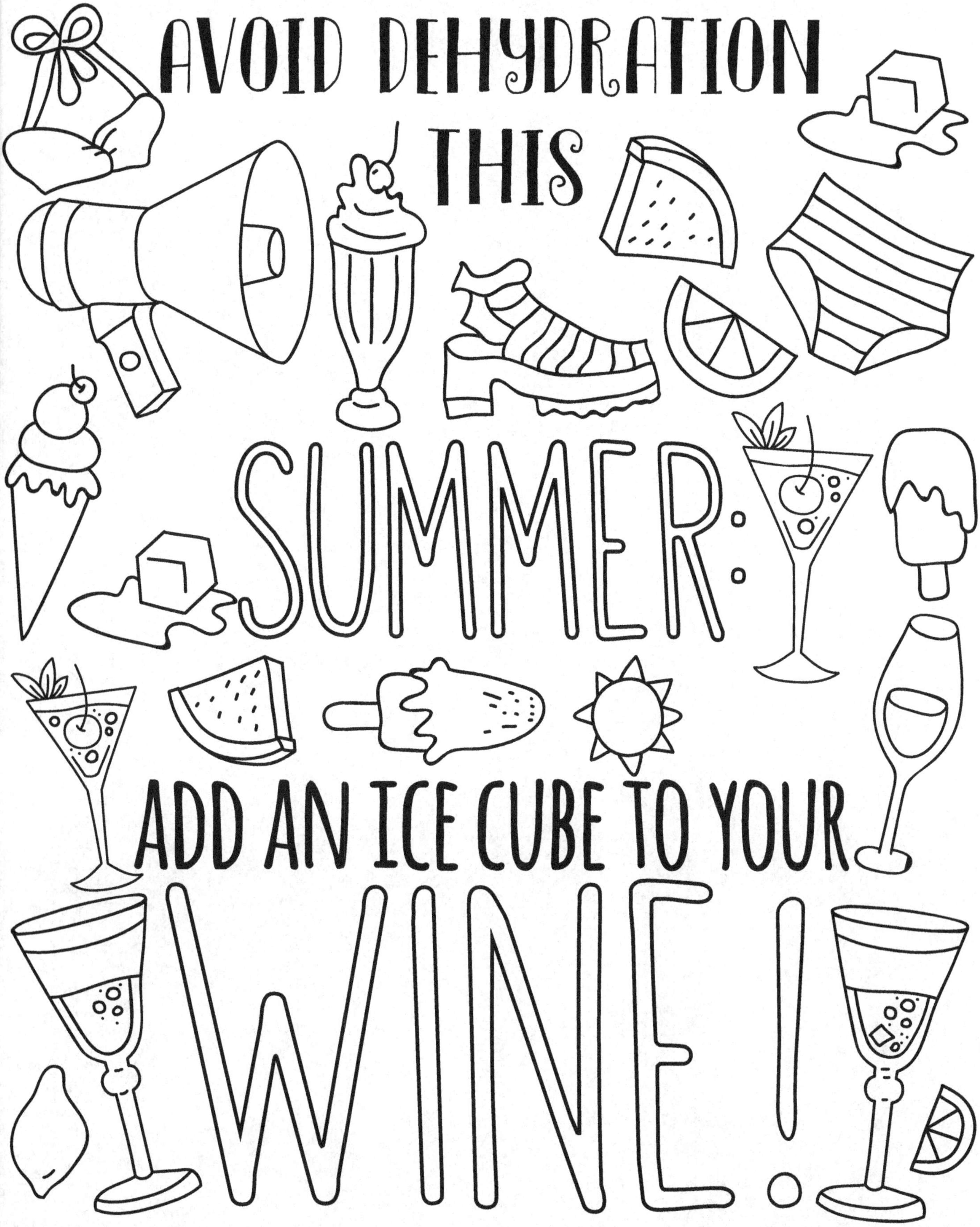
AVOID DEHYDRATION
THIS
SUMMER:
ADD AN ICE CUBE TO YOUR
WINE!

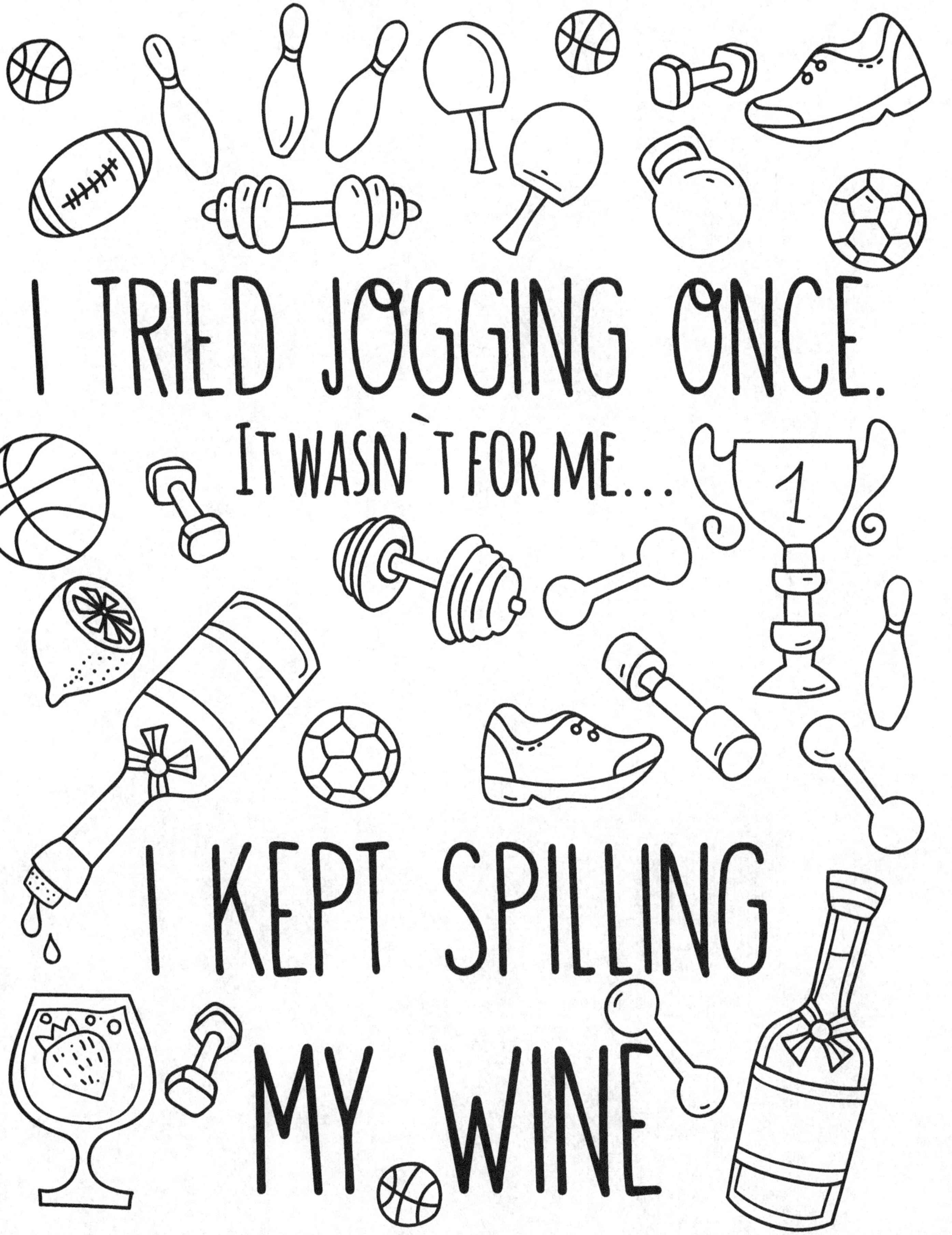
I TRIED JOGGING ONCE.
IT WASN`T FOR ME...
1
I KEPT SPILLING
MY WINE

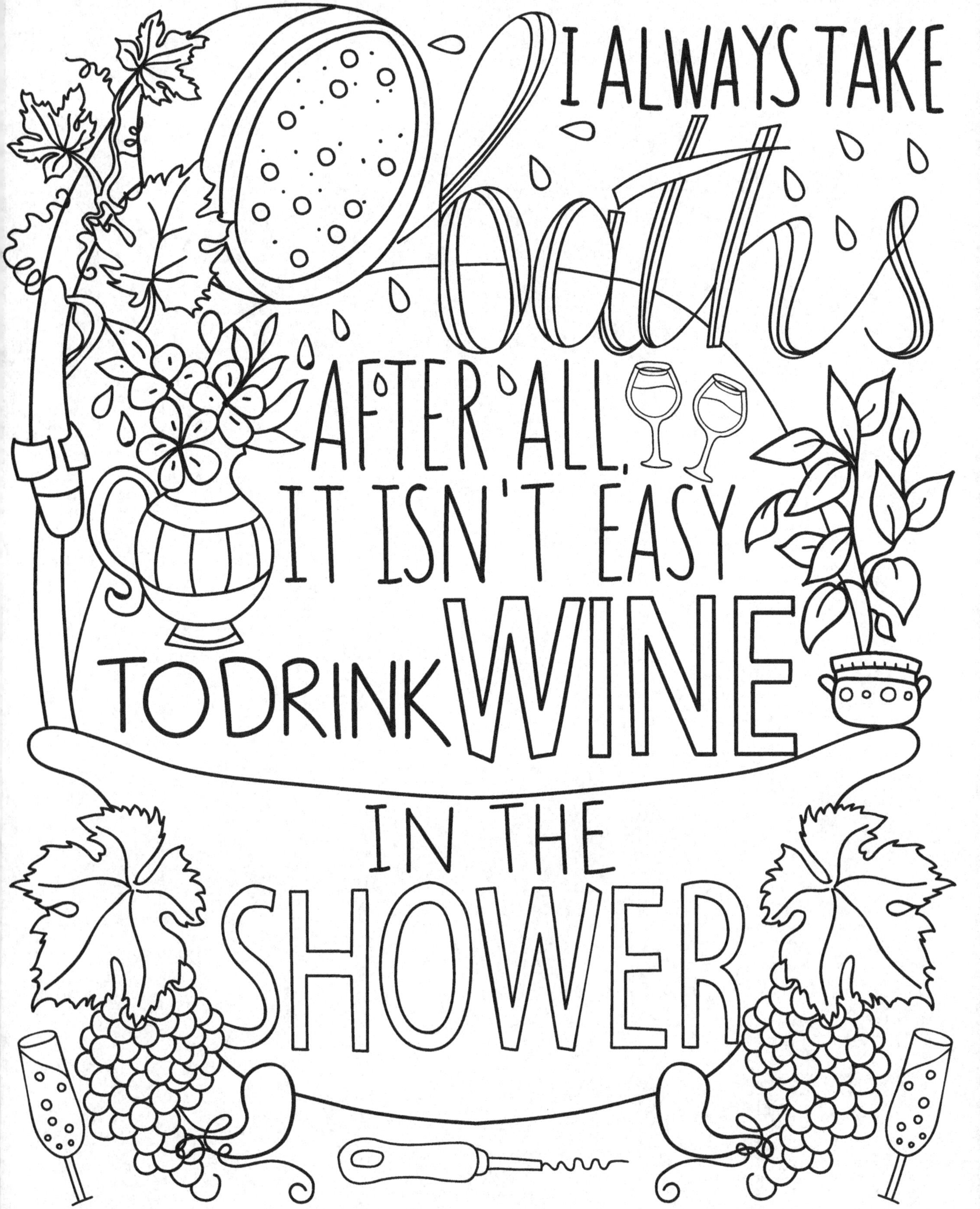
I ALWAYS TAKE
baths
AFTER ALL,
IT ISN'T EASY
TO DRINK WINE
IN THE
SHOWER

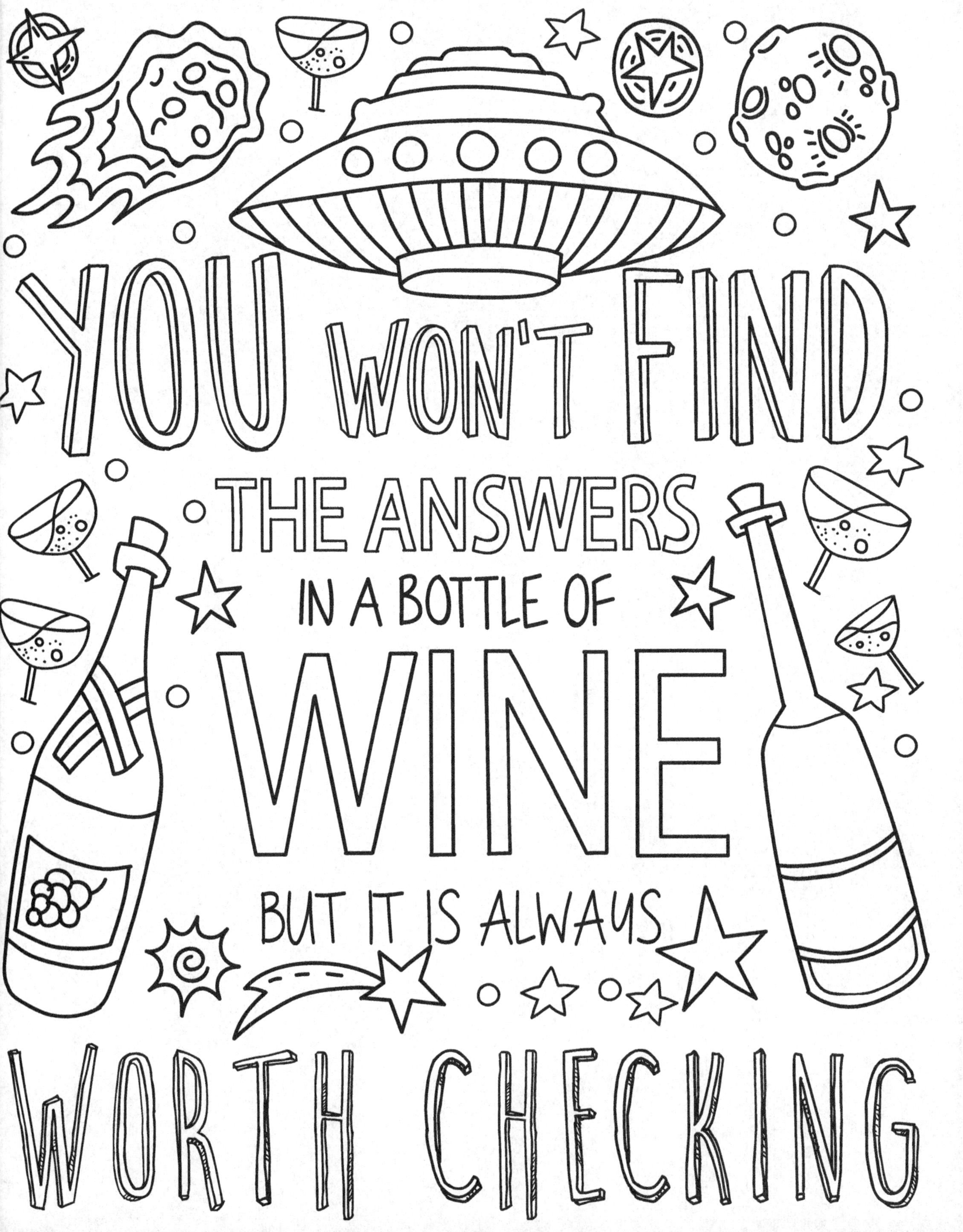
YOU WON'T FIND
THE ANSWERS
IN A BOTTLE OF
WINE
BUT IT IS ALWAYS
WORTH CHECKING

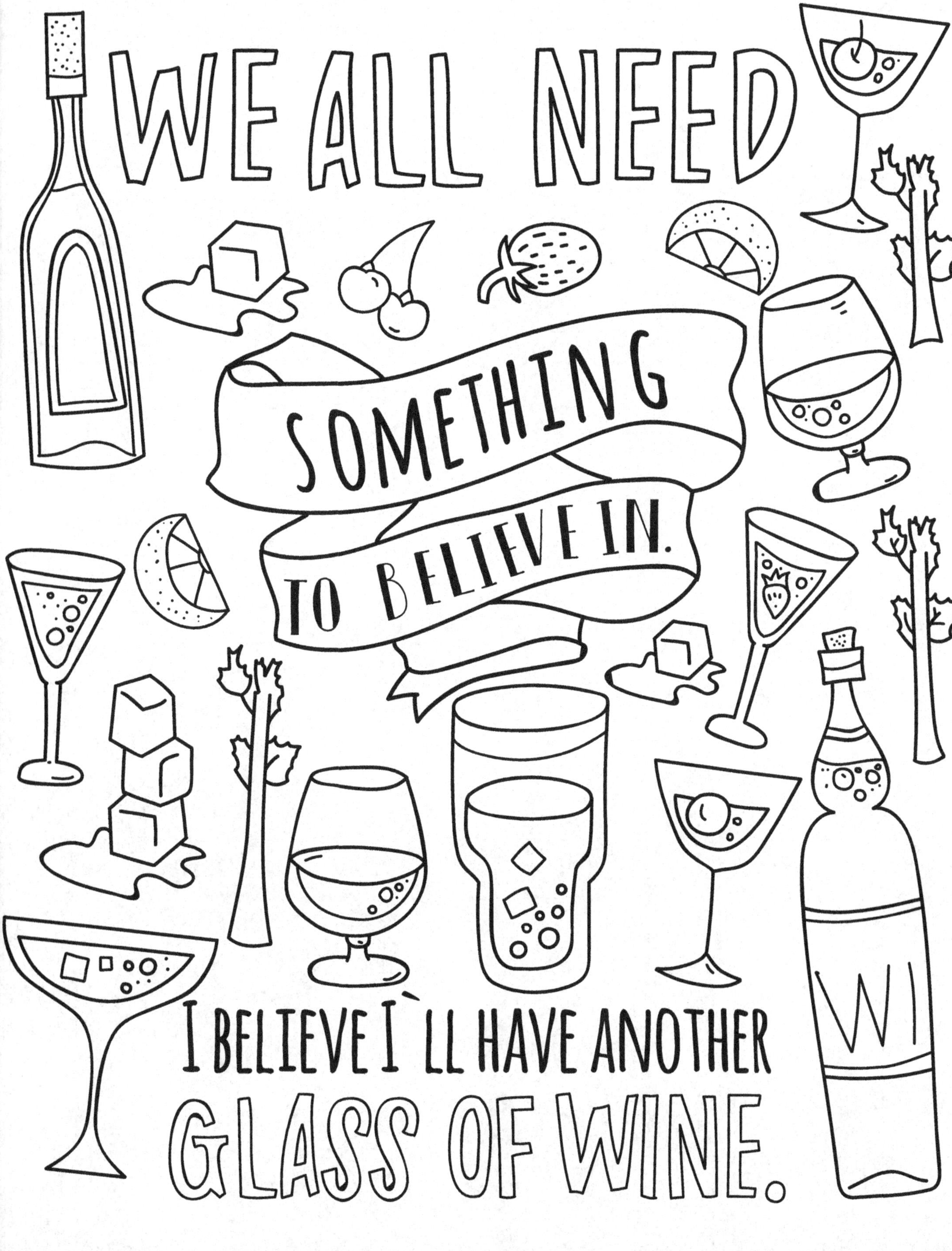
WE ALL NEED
SOMETHING
TO BELIEVE IN.
I BELIEVE I`LL HAVE ANOTHER
GLASS OF WINE.
WI

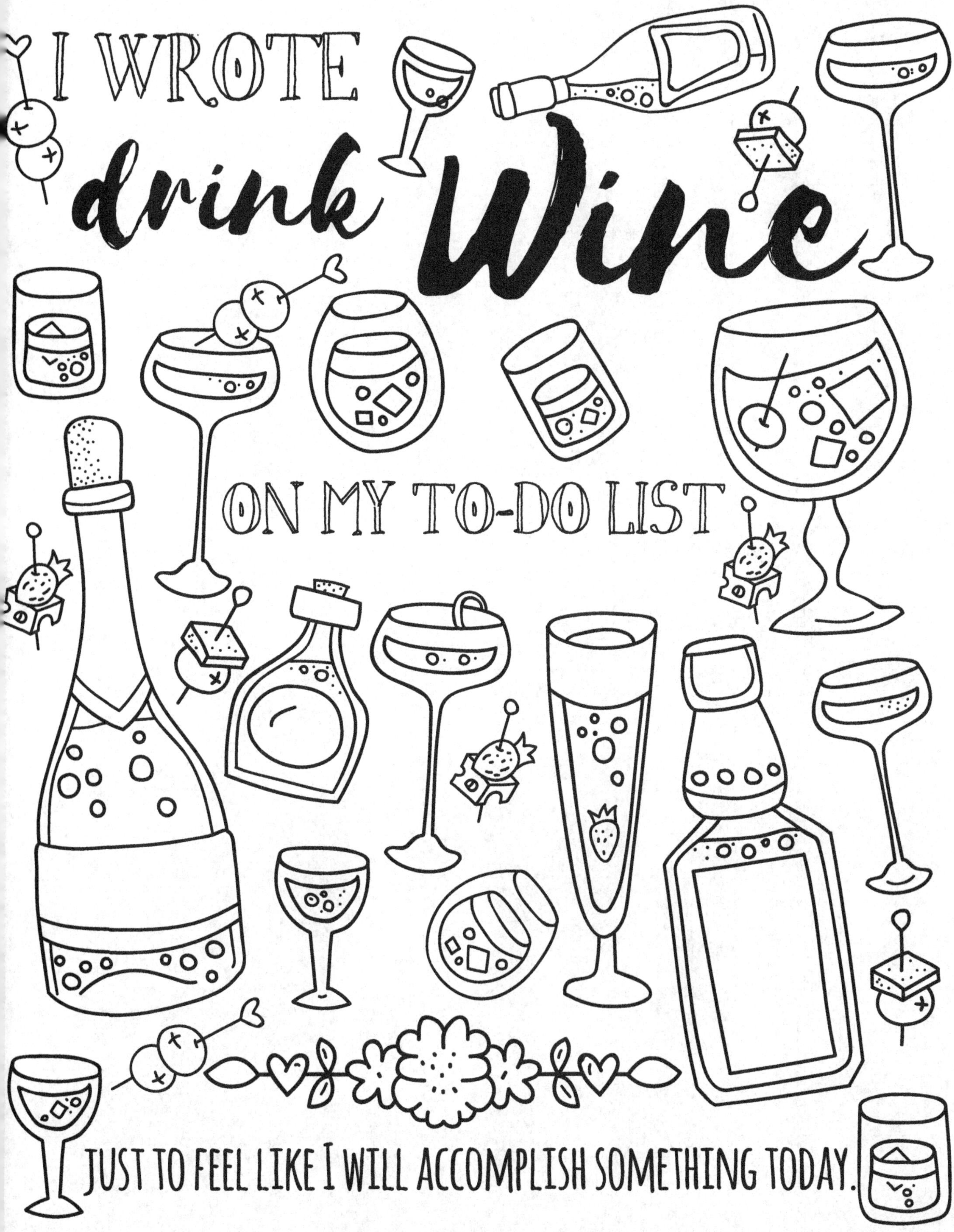
I WROTE
drink Wine
ON MY TO-DO LIST
JUST TO FEEL LIKE I WILL ACCOMPLISH SOMETHING TODAY.

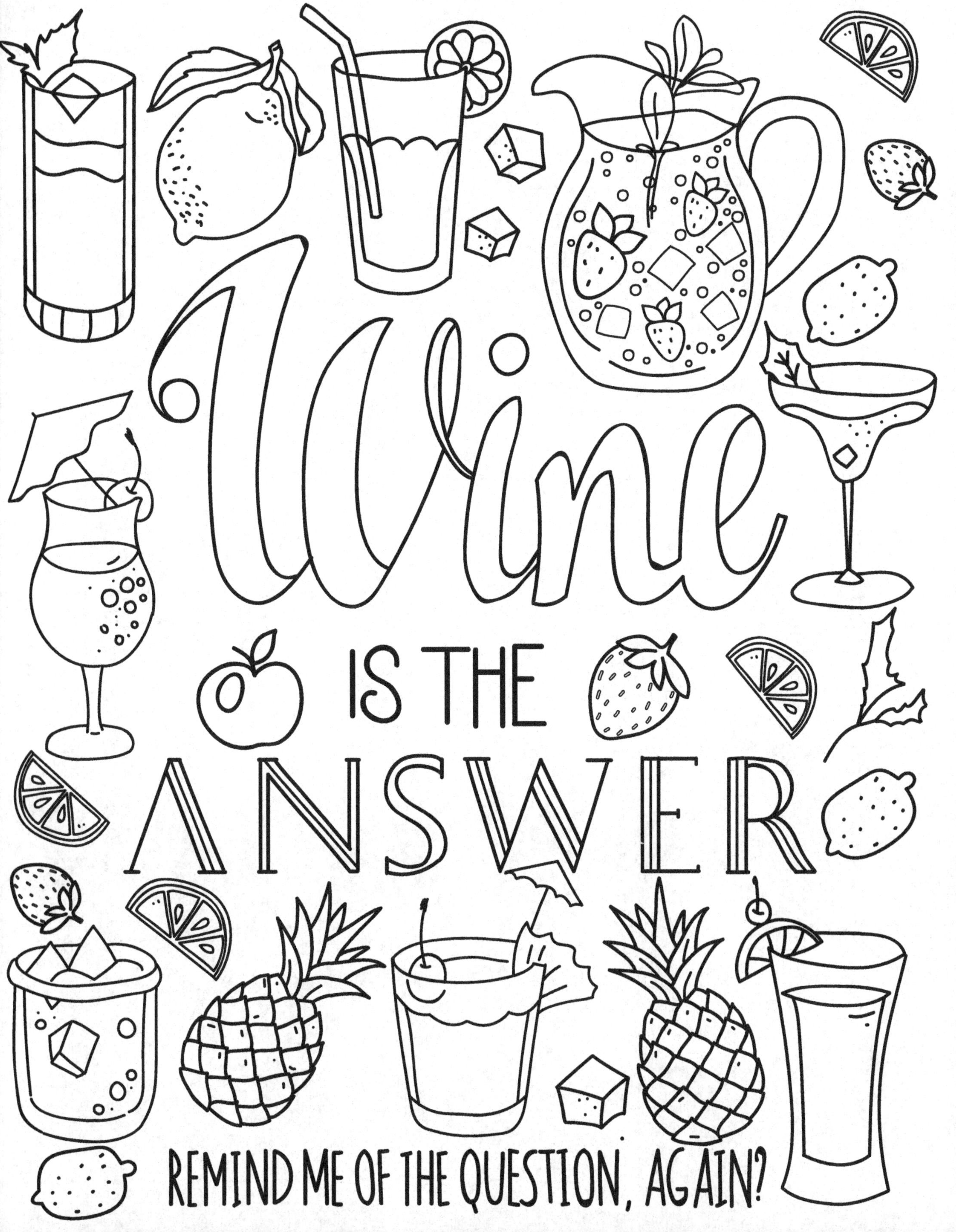
Wine
IS THE
ANSWER
REMIND ME OF THE QUESTION, AGAIN?

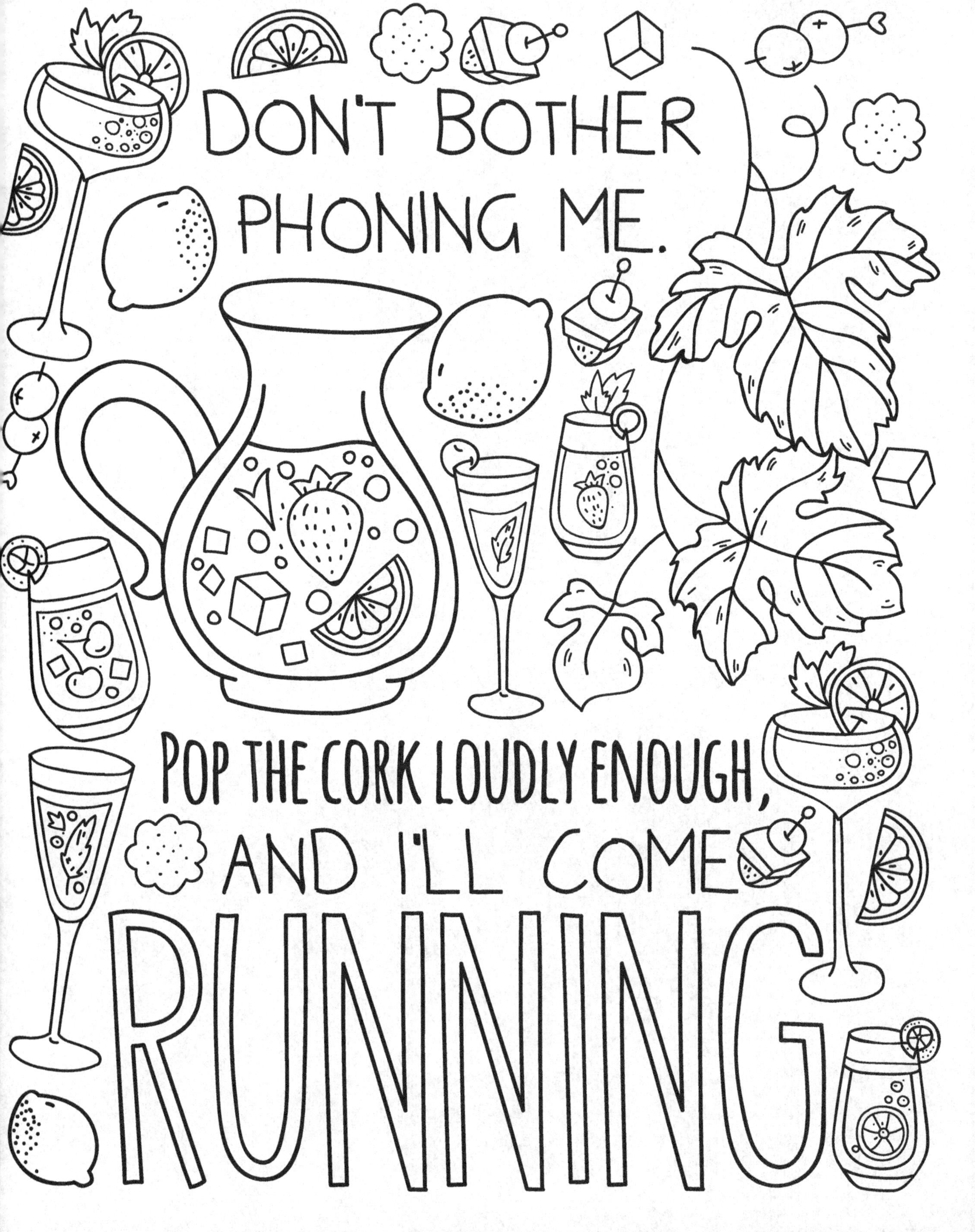
DON'T BOTHER
PHONING ME.
POP THE CORK LOUDLY ENOUGH,
AND I'LL COME
RUNNING

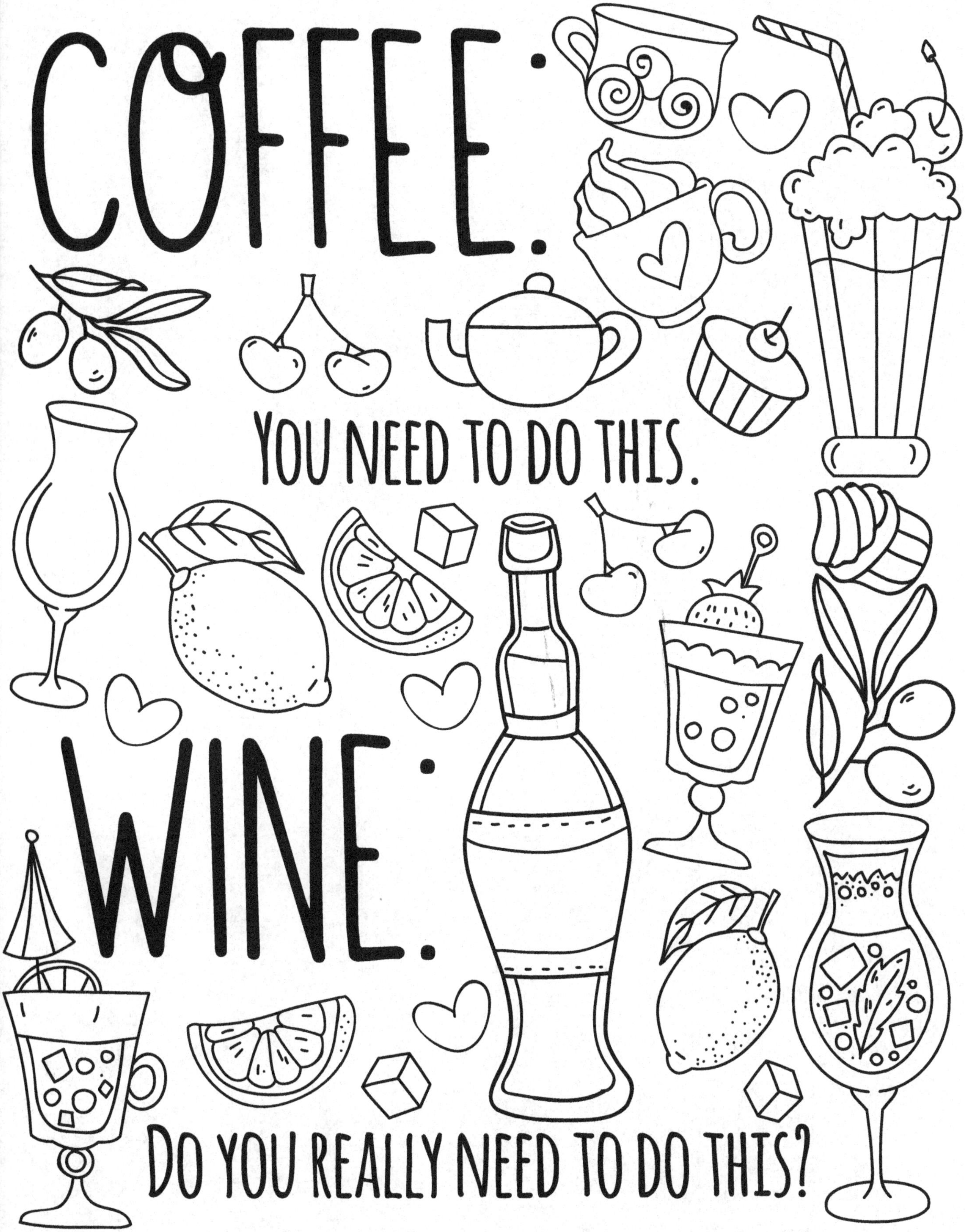
COFFEE:
YOU NEED TO DO THIS.
WINE:
DO YOU REALLY NEED TO DO THIS?

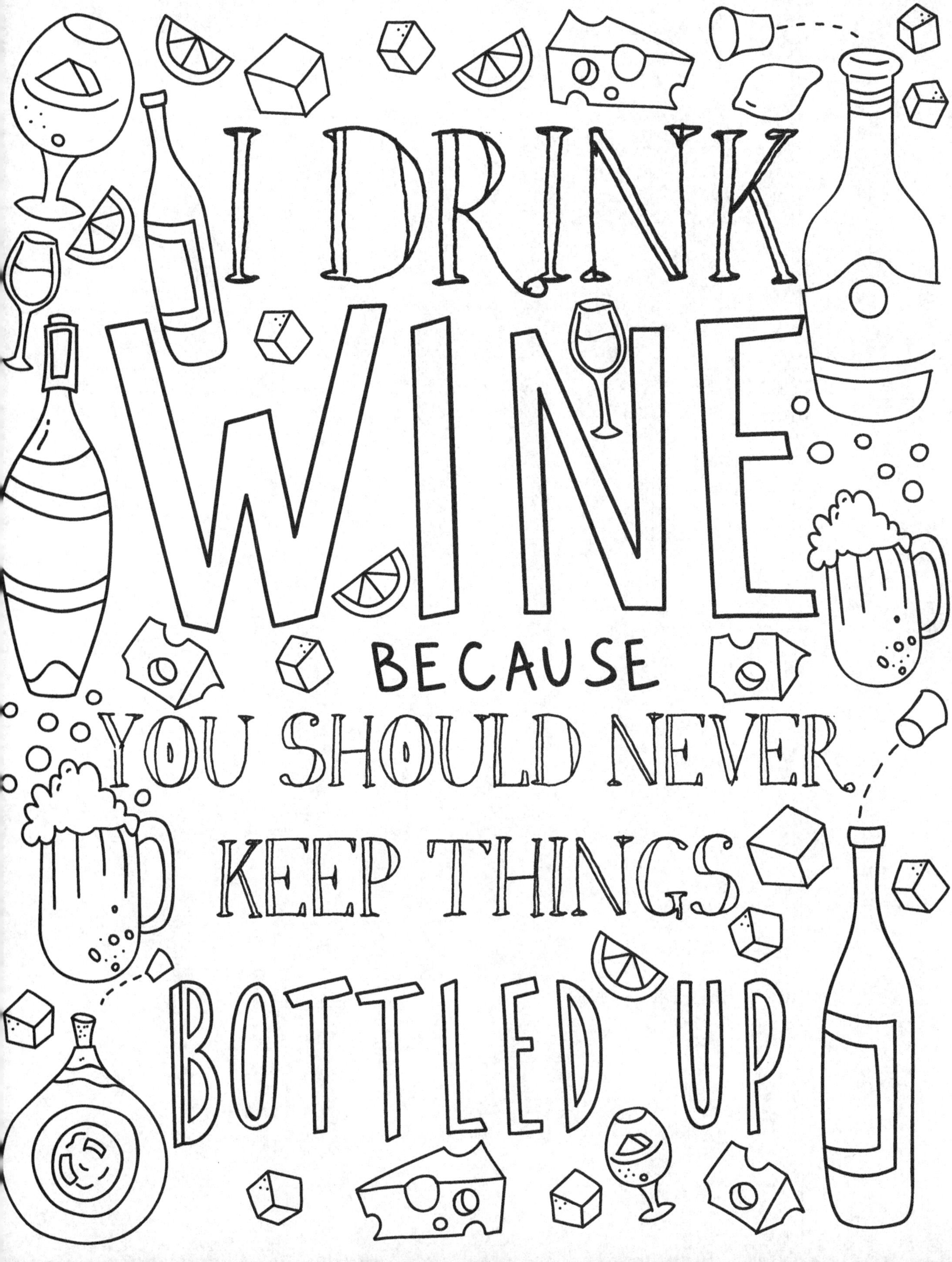
I DRINK
WINE
BECAUSE
YOU SHOULD NEVER
KEEP THINGS
BOTTLED UP

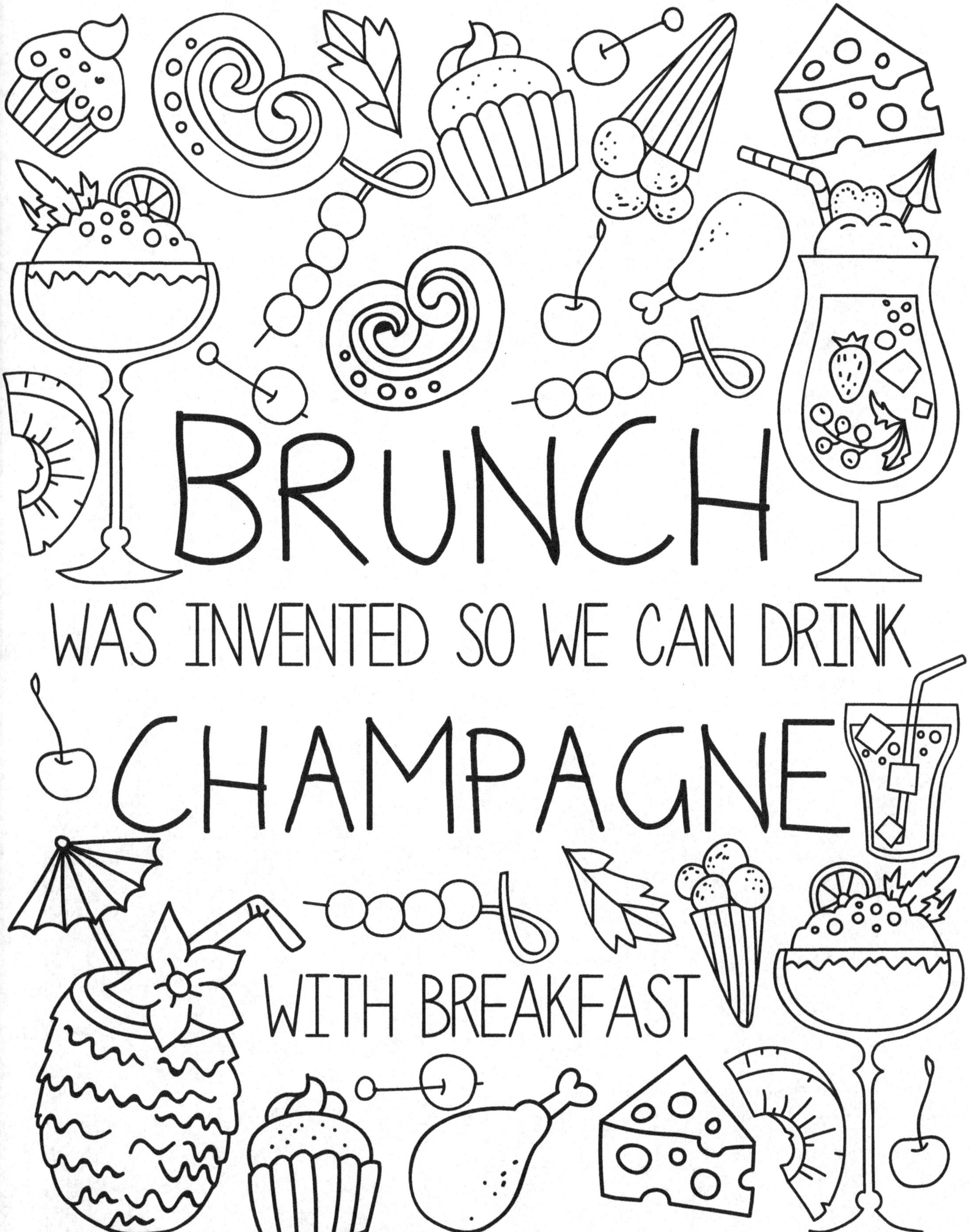
BRUNCH
WAS INVENTED SO WE CAN DRINK
CHAMPAGNE
WITH BREAKFAST

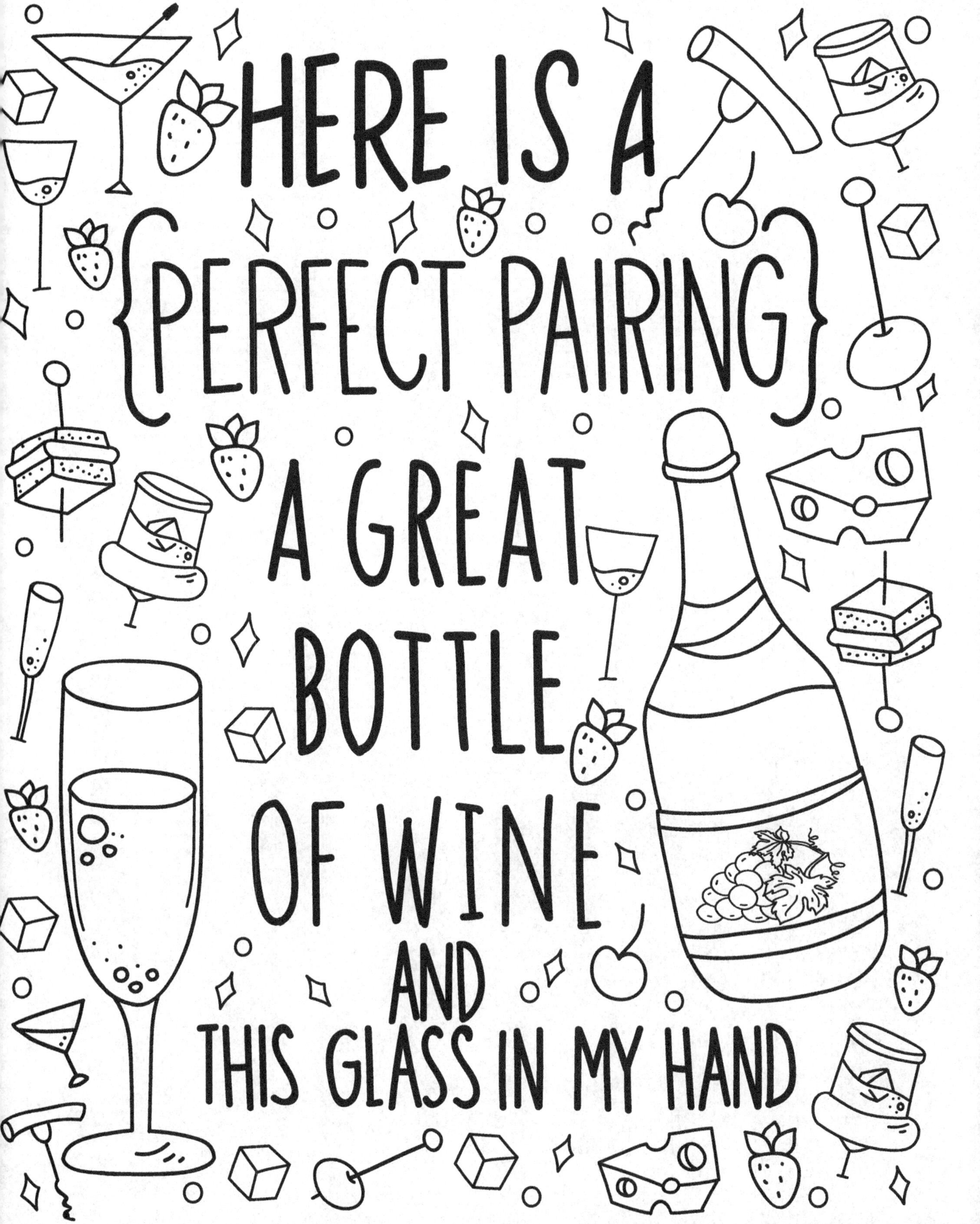
HERE IS A
PERFECT PAIRING
A GREAT
BOTTLE
OF WINE
AND
THIS GLASS IN MY HAND

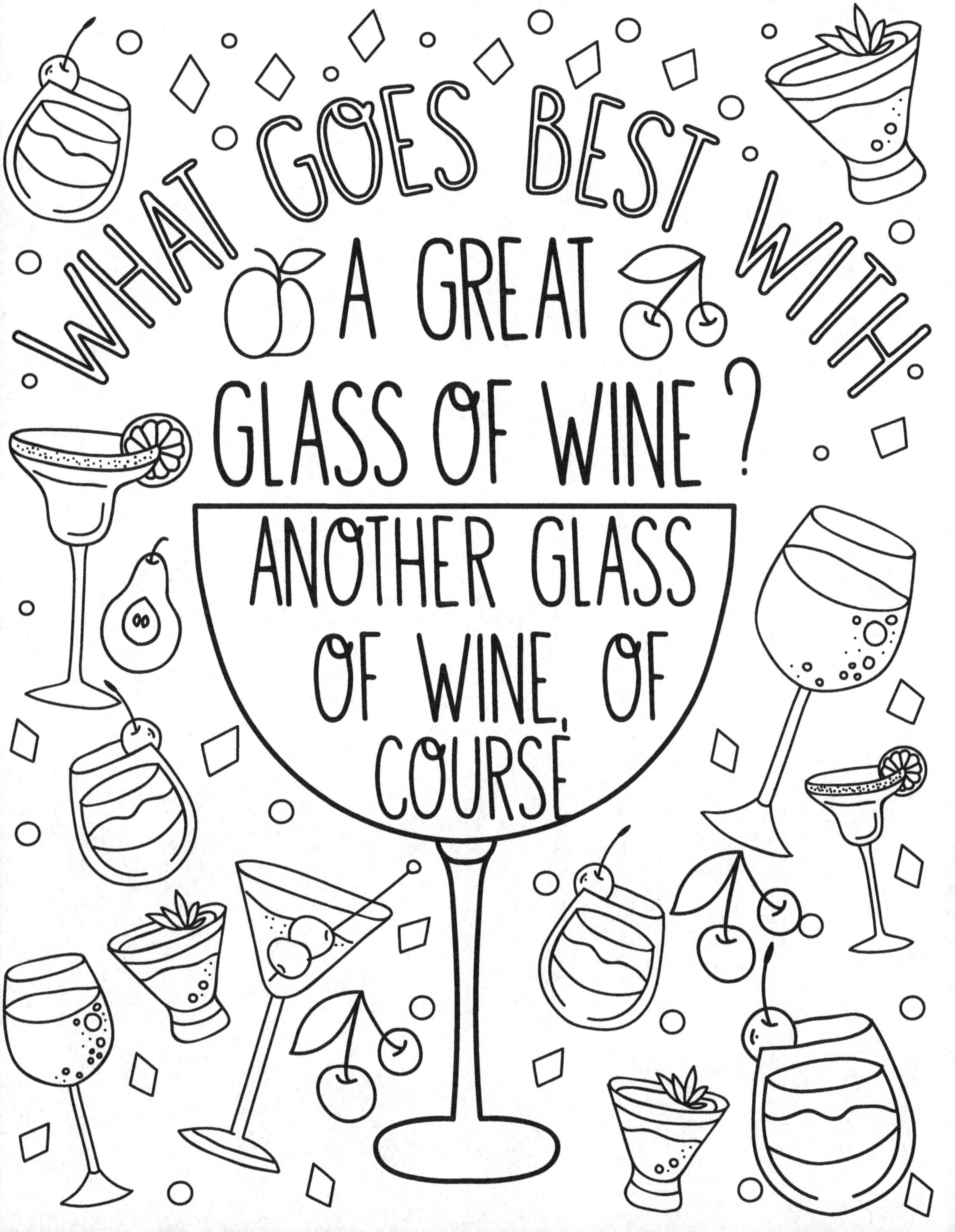
WHAT GOES BEST WITH
A GREAT
GLASS OF WINE?
ANOTHER GLASS
OF WINE, OF
COURSE

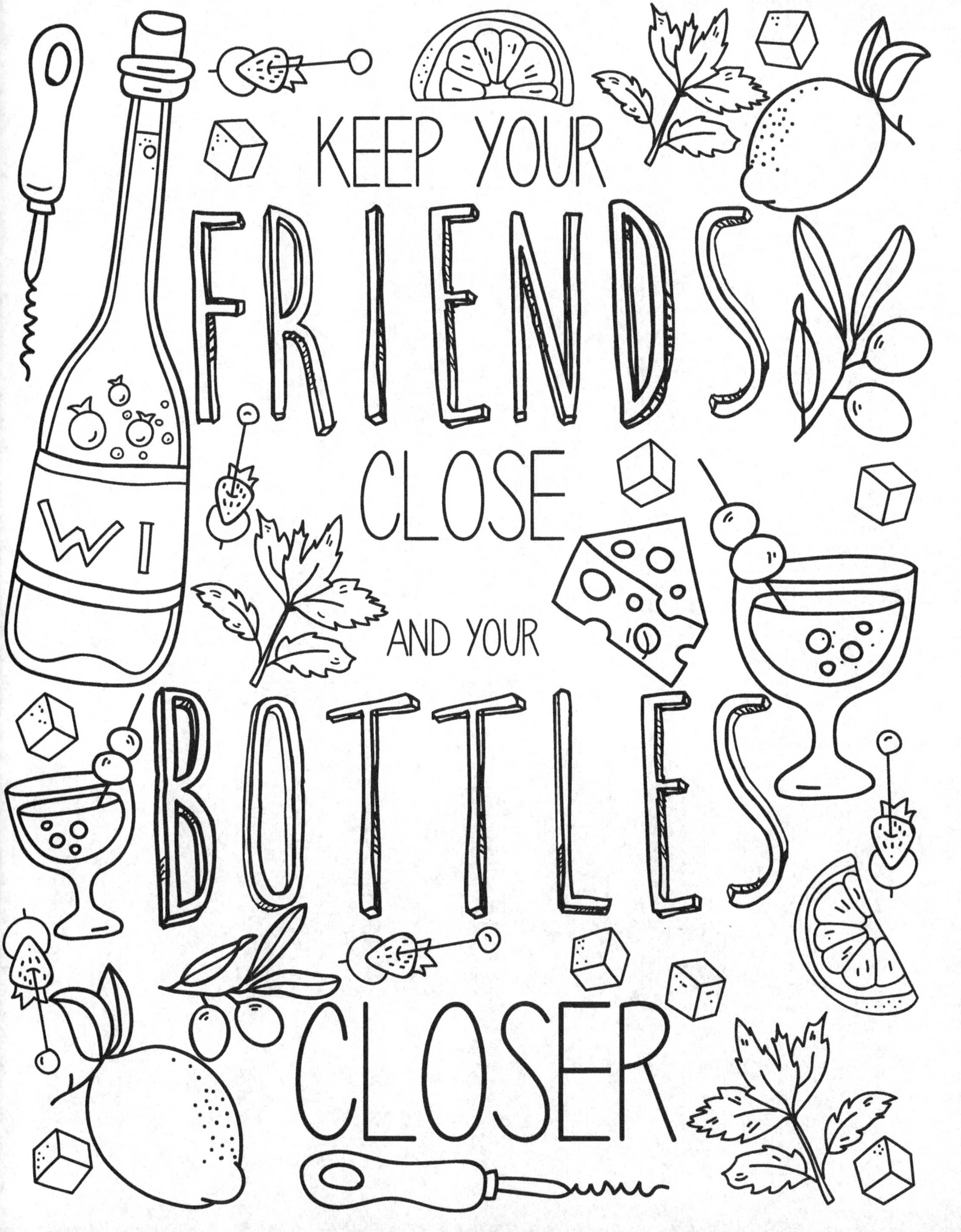
KEEP YOUR
FRIENDS
CLOSE
AND YOUR
BOTTLES
CLOSER

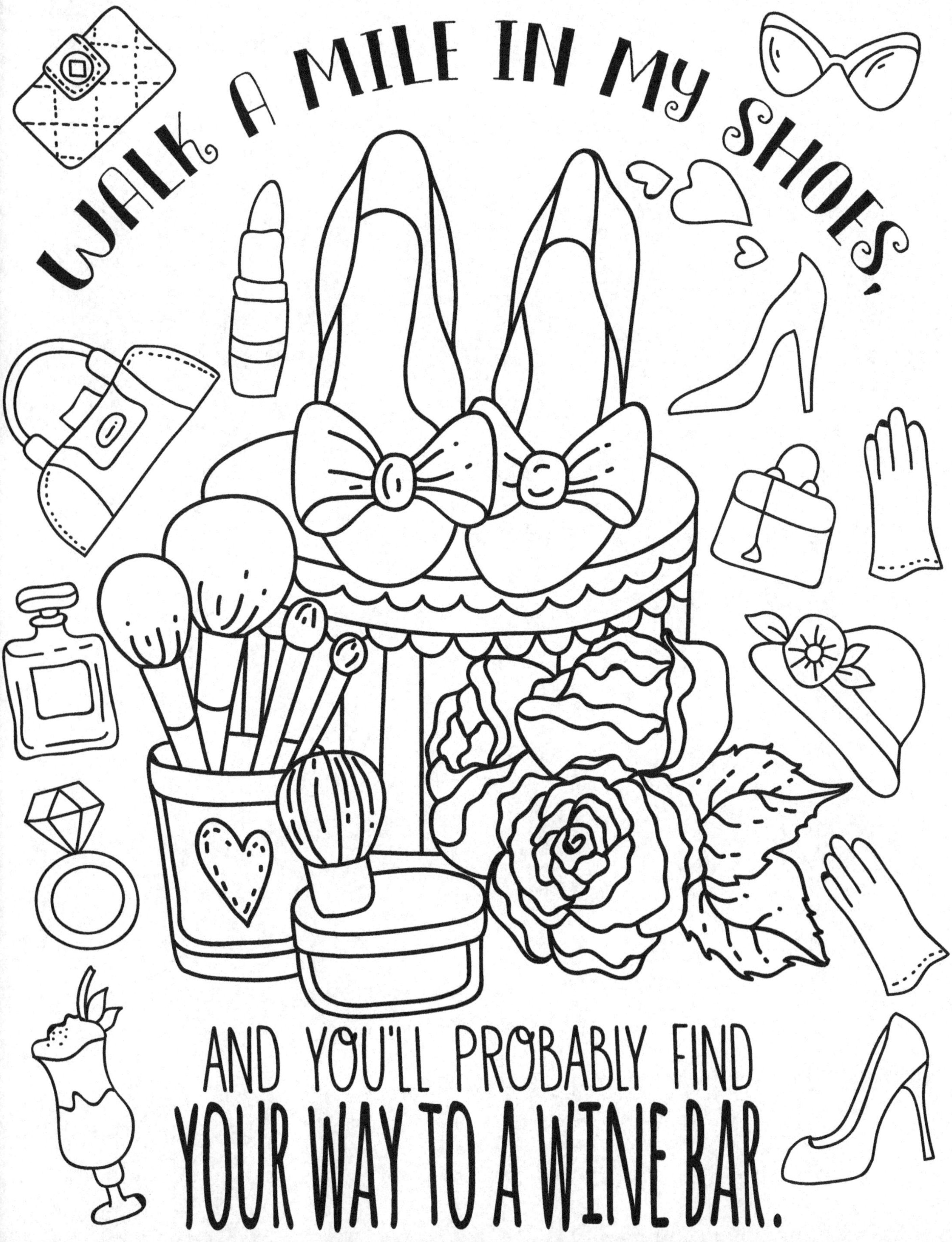
WALK A MILE IN MY SHOES,
AND YOU'LL PROBABLY FIND
YOUR WAY TO A WINE BAR.

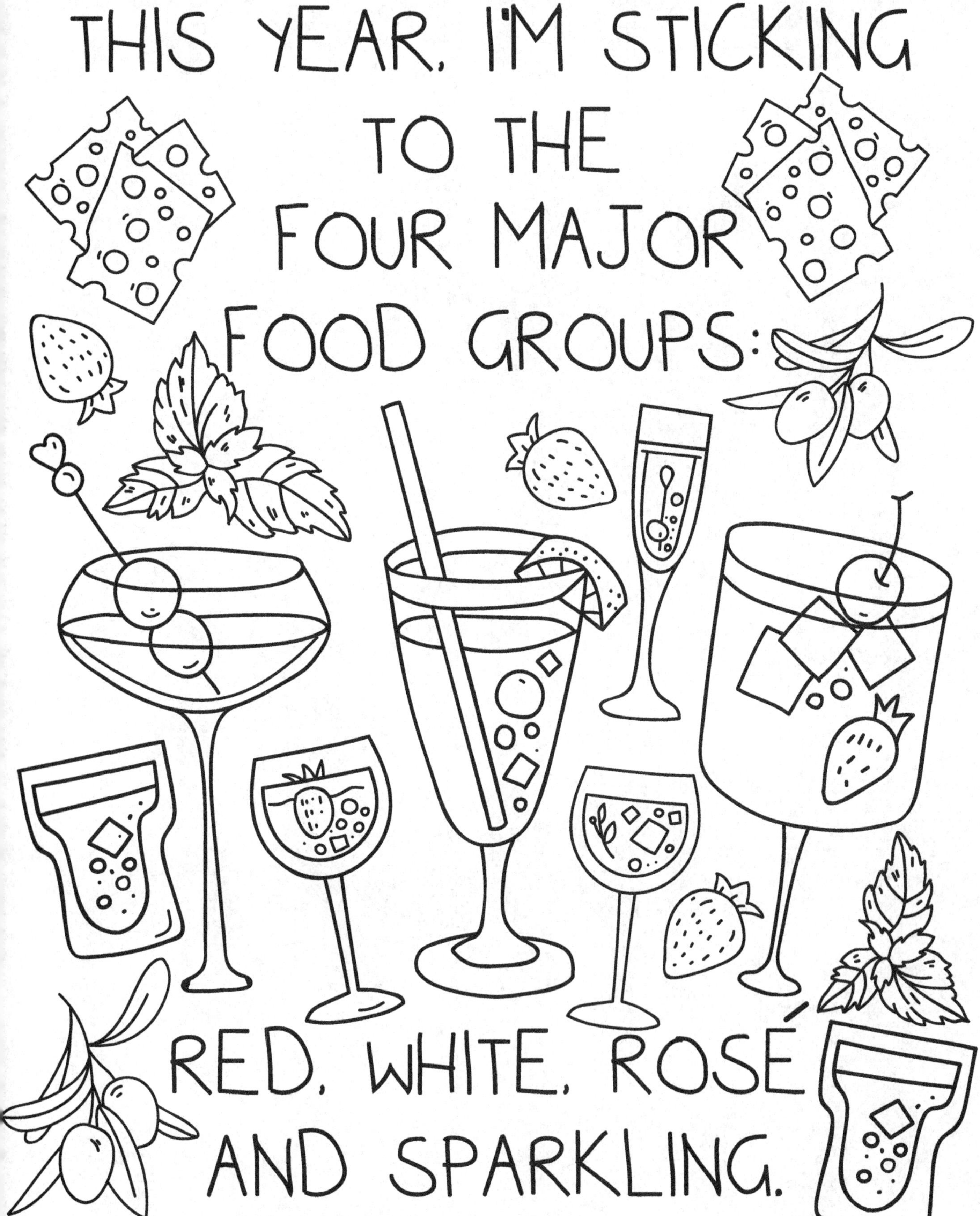
THIS YEAR, I'M STICKING TO THE FOUR MAJOR FOOD GROUPS:
RED, WHITE, ROSÉ AND SPARKLING.

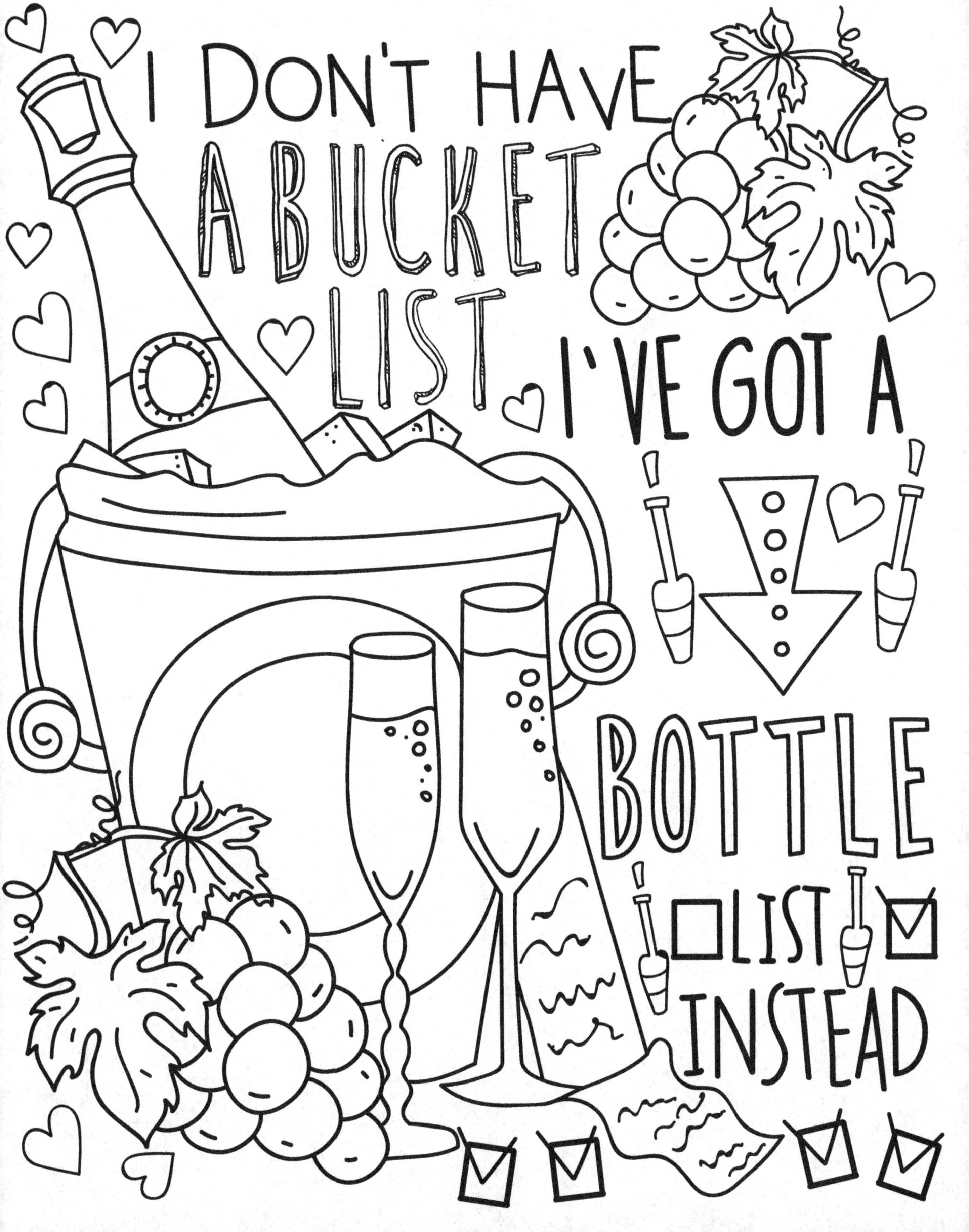

I DON'T HAVE
A BUCKET
LIST
I'VE GOT A
BOTTLE
LIST
INSTEAD

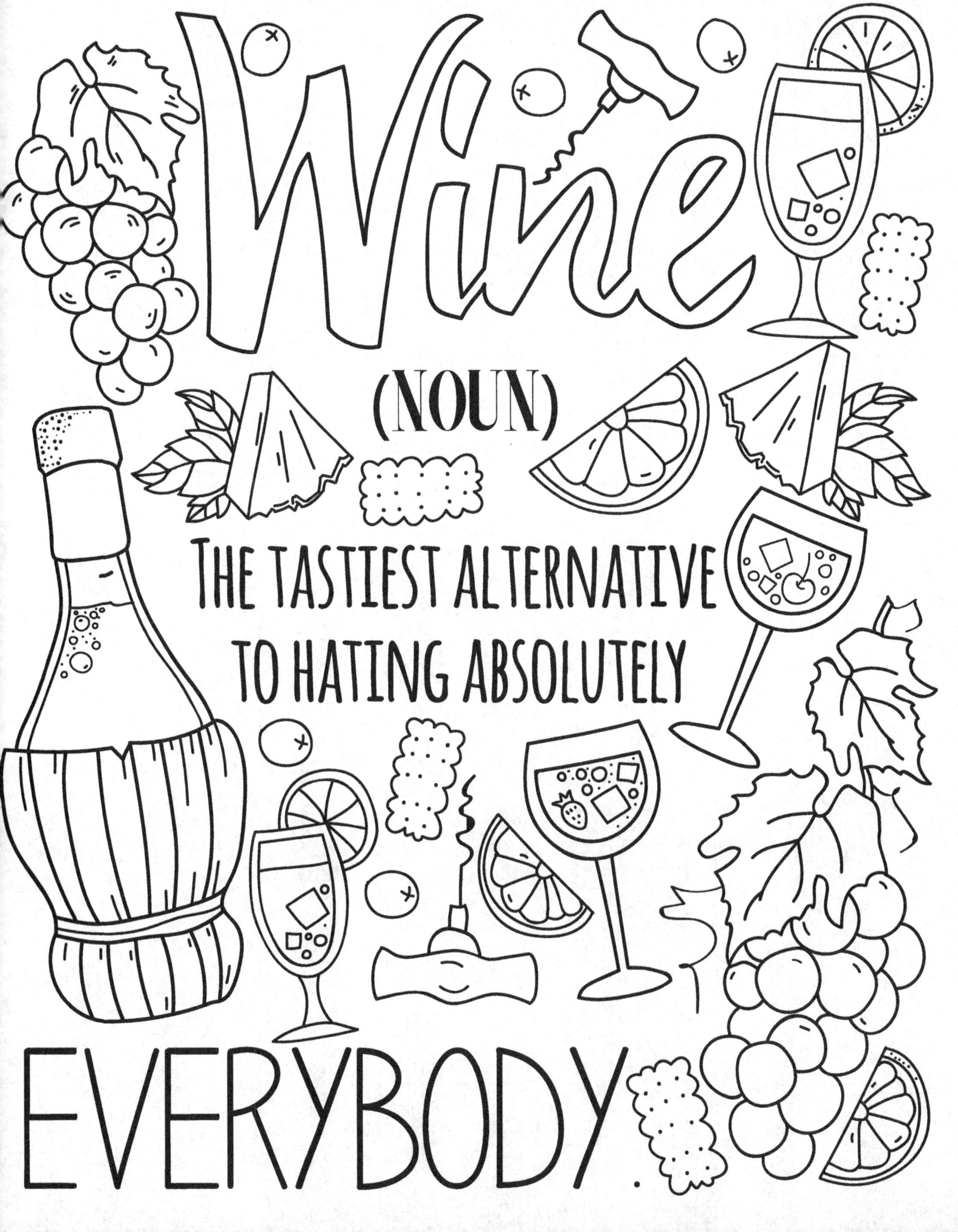
Wine
(NOUN)
THE TASTIEST ALTERNATIVE
TO HATING ABSOLUTELY
EVERYBODY.

I'VE ALWAYS CONSIDERED MYSELF AN OUTDOORS PERSON AFTER ALL; I LOVE DRINKING WINE IN MY GARDEN

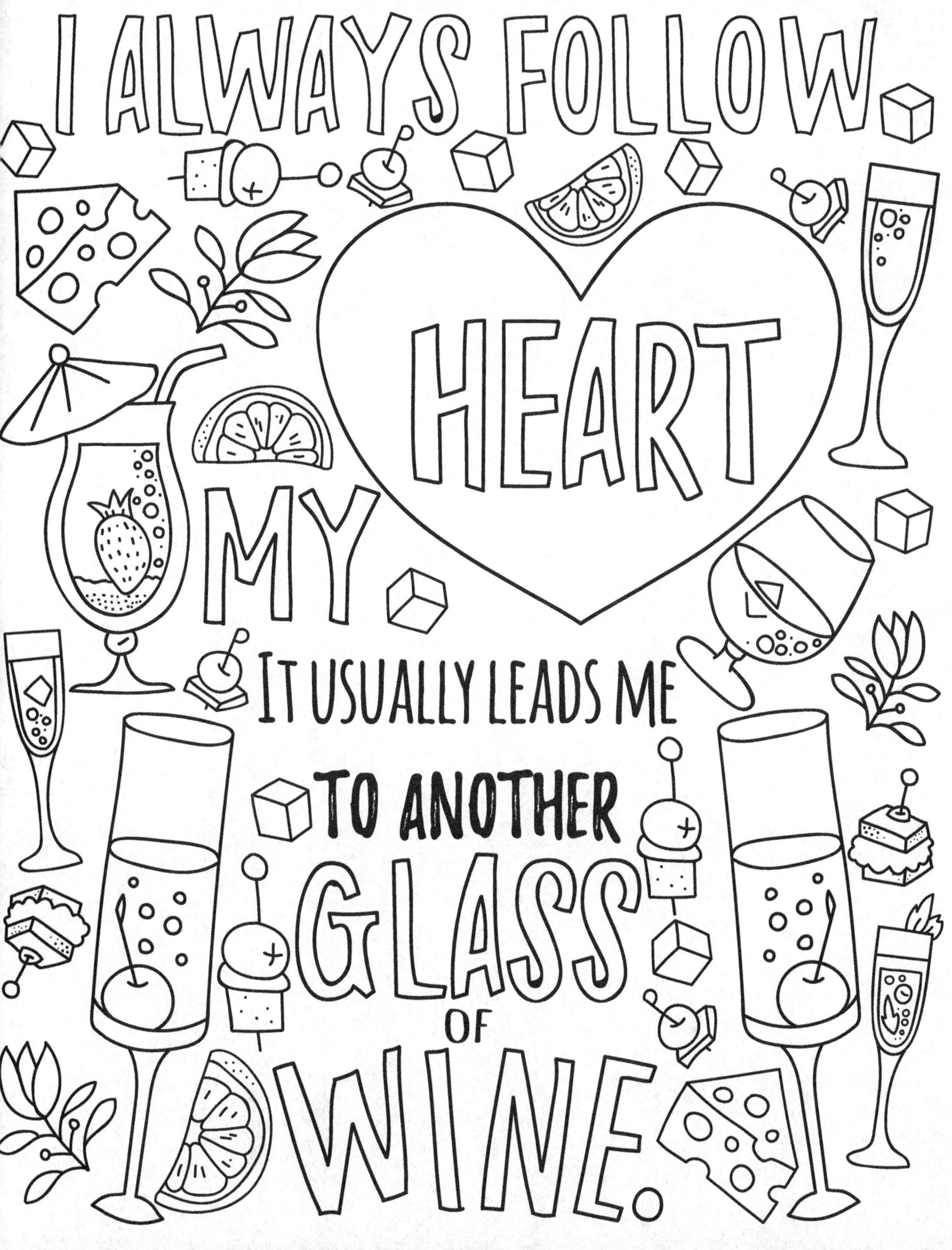
I ALWAYS FOLLOW
MY
HEART
IT USUALLY LEADS ME
TO ANOTHER
GLASS
OF
WINE.

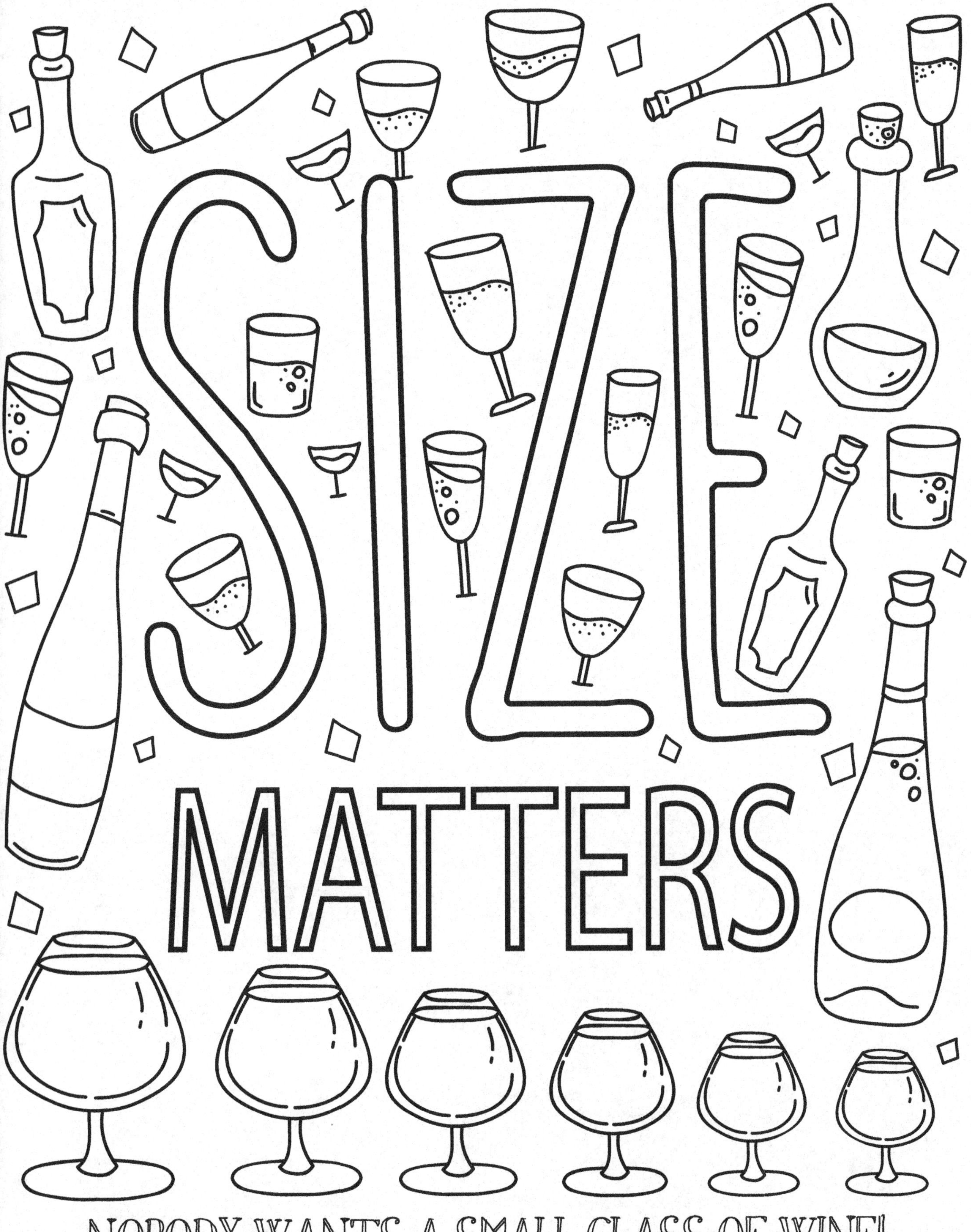

NOBODY WANTS A SMALL GLASS OF WINE!

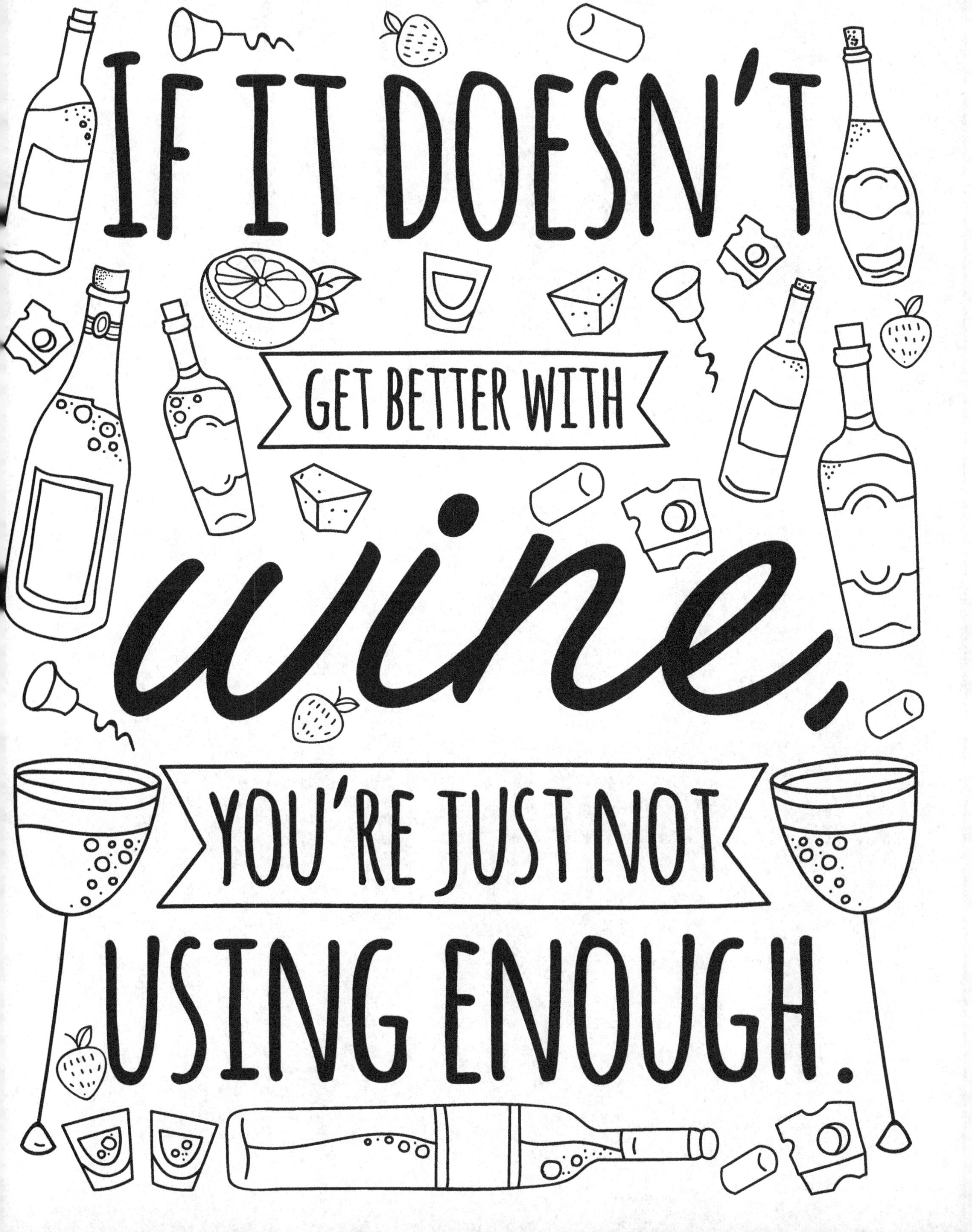
IF IT DOESN'T
GET BETTER WITH
wine,
YOU'RE JUST NOT
USING ENOUGH.

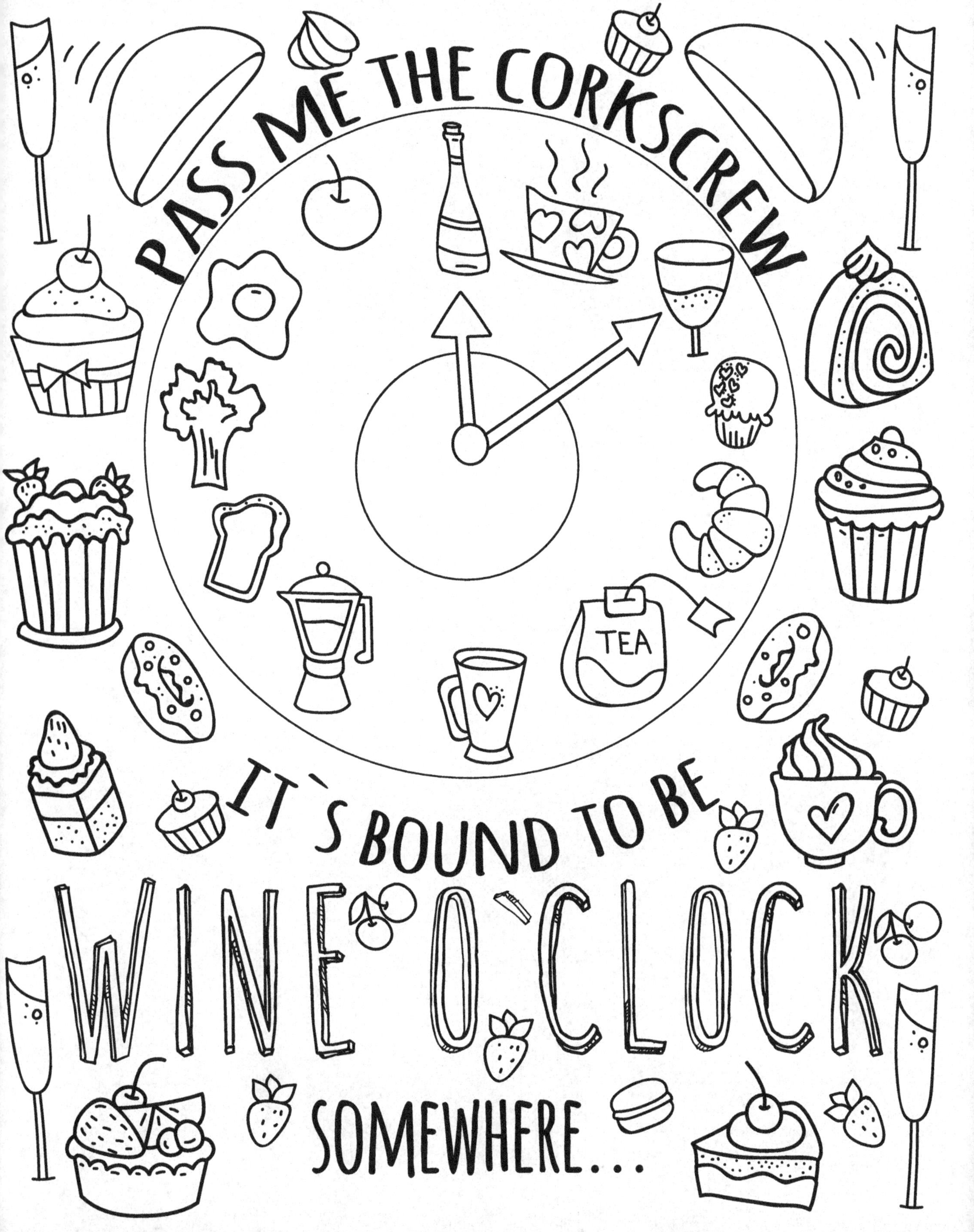
PASS ME THE CORKSCREW
TEA
IT`S BOUND TO BE
WINE O`CLOCK
SOMEWHERE...

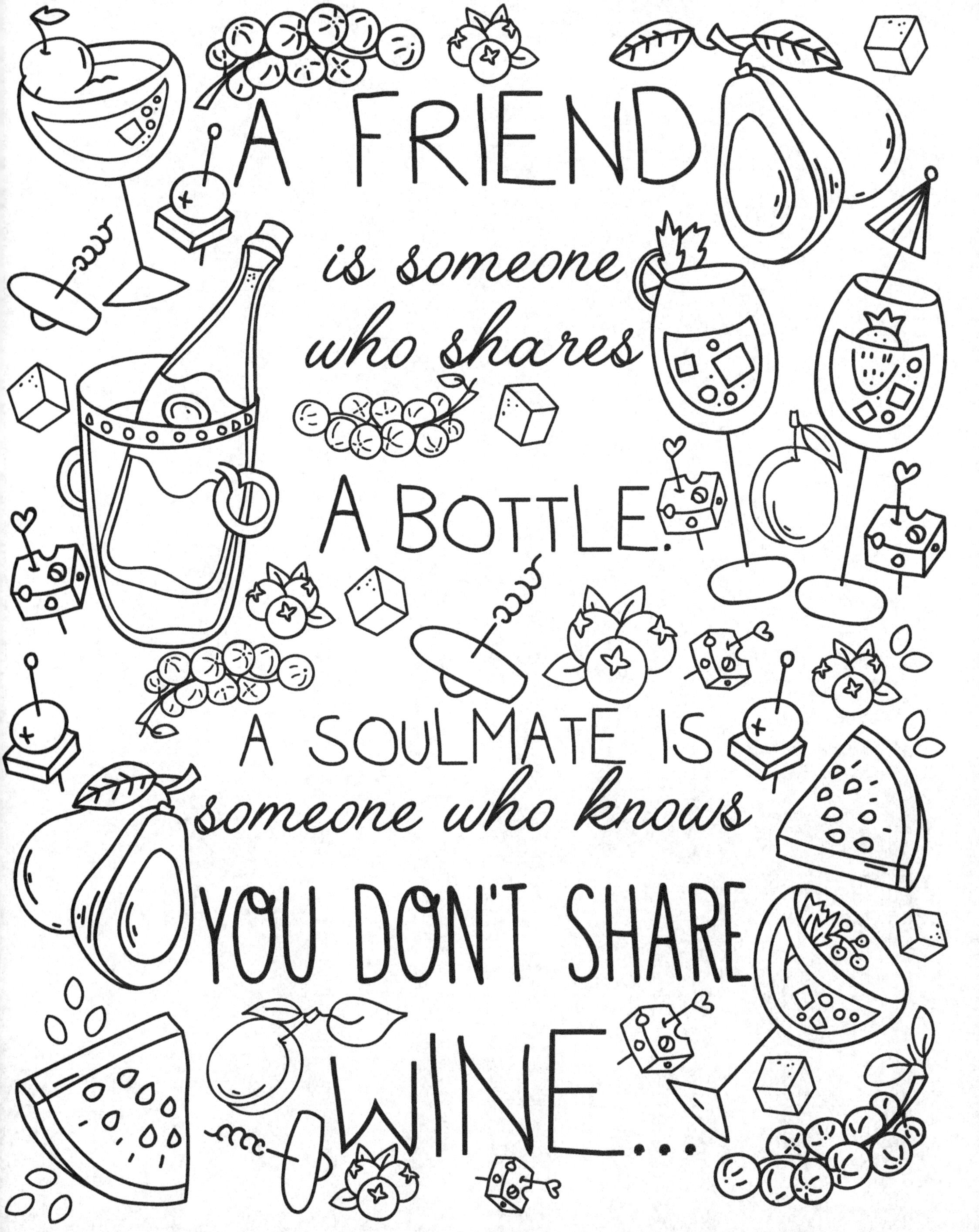
A FRIEND
is someone
who shares
A BOTTLE.
A SOULMATE IS
someone who knows
YOU DON'T SHARE
WINE...

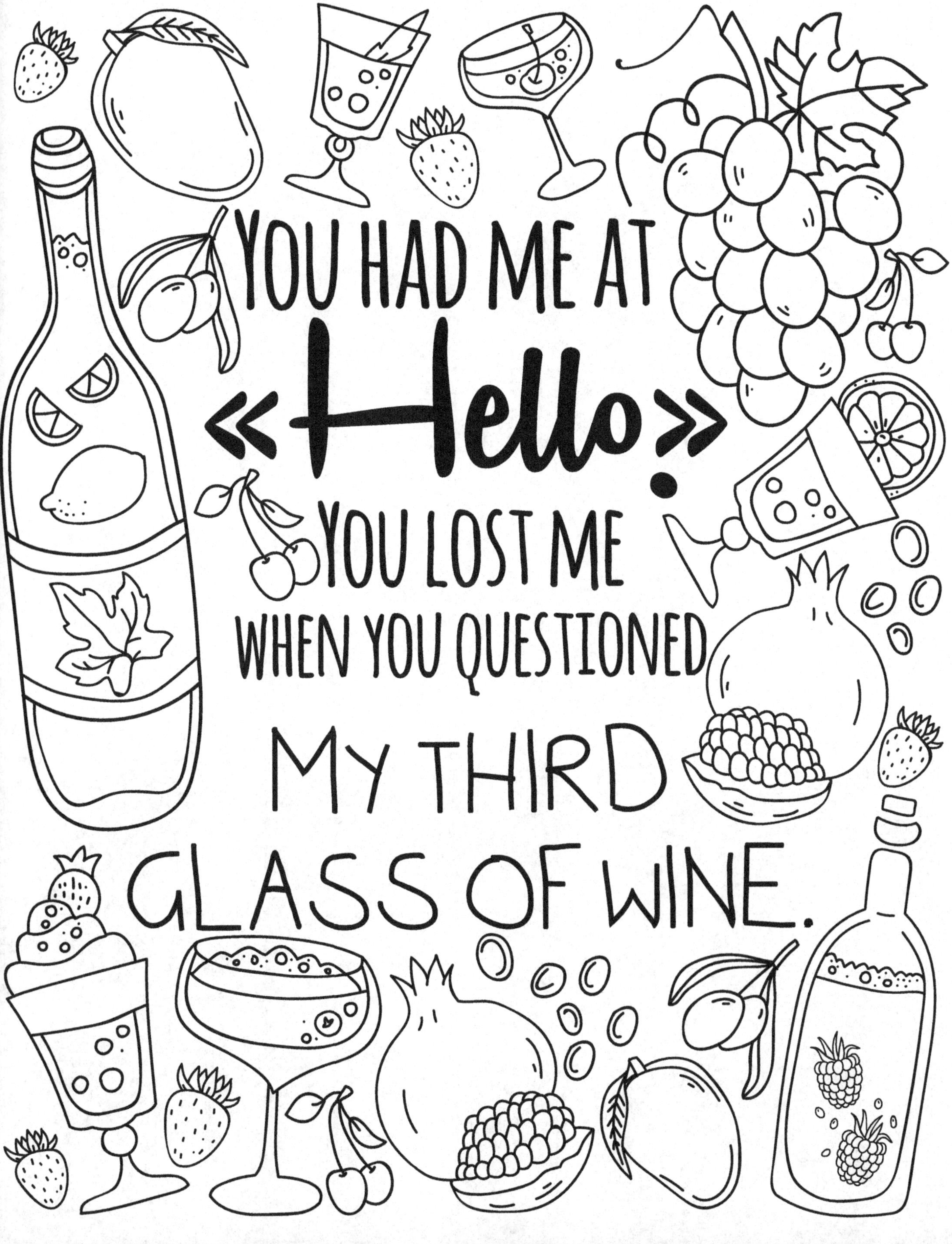
YOU HAD ME AT
«Hello»
YOU LOST ME
WHEN YOU QUESTIONED
MY THIRD
GLASS OF WINE.

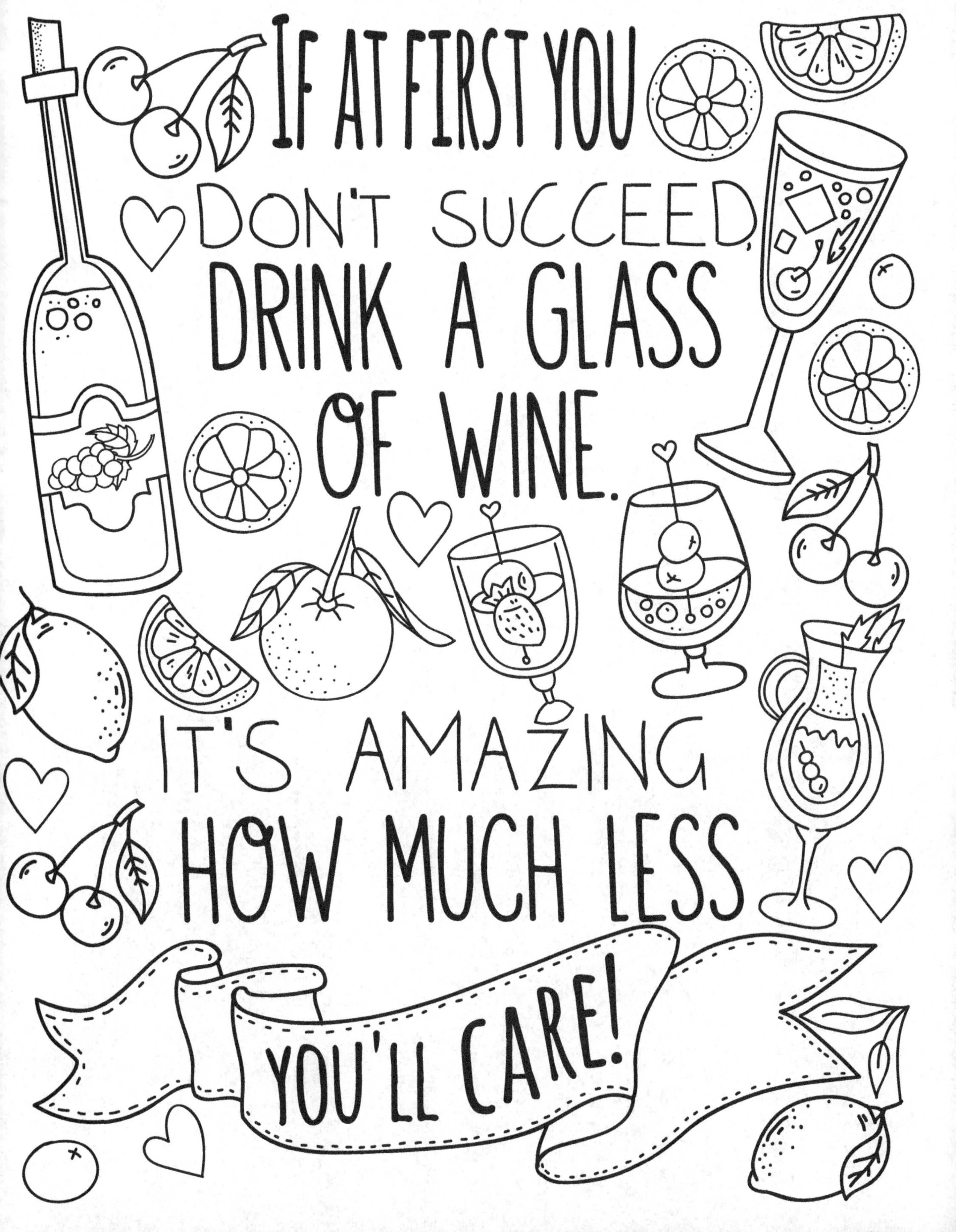
IF AT FIRST YOU
DON'T SUCCEED,
DRINK A GLASS
OF WINE.
IT'S AMAZING
HOW MUCH LESS
YOU'LL CARE!

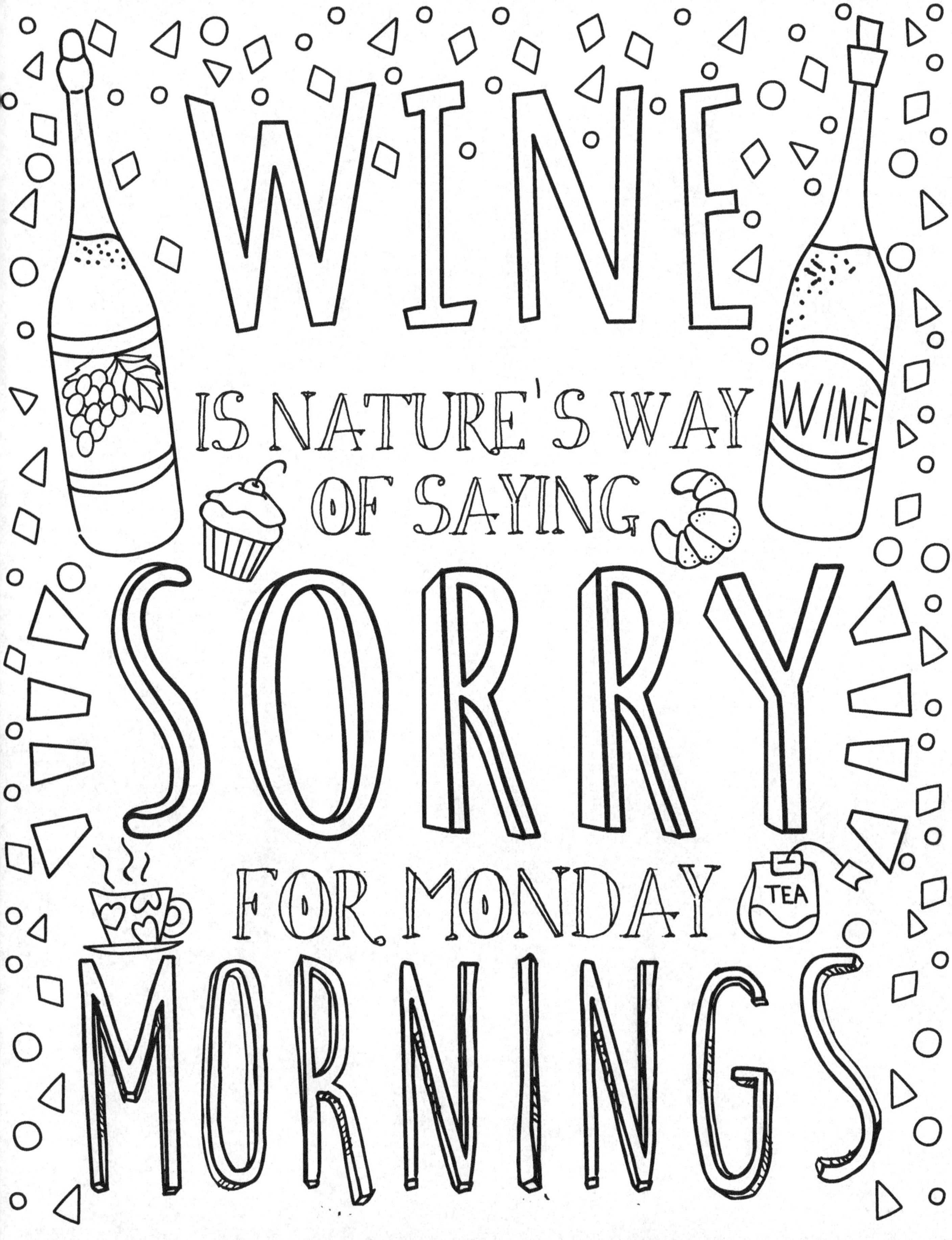
WINE
IS NATURE'S WAY
OF SAYING
SORRY
FOR MONDAY
MORNINGS
WINE
TEA

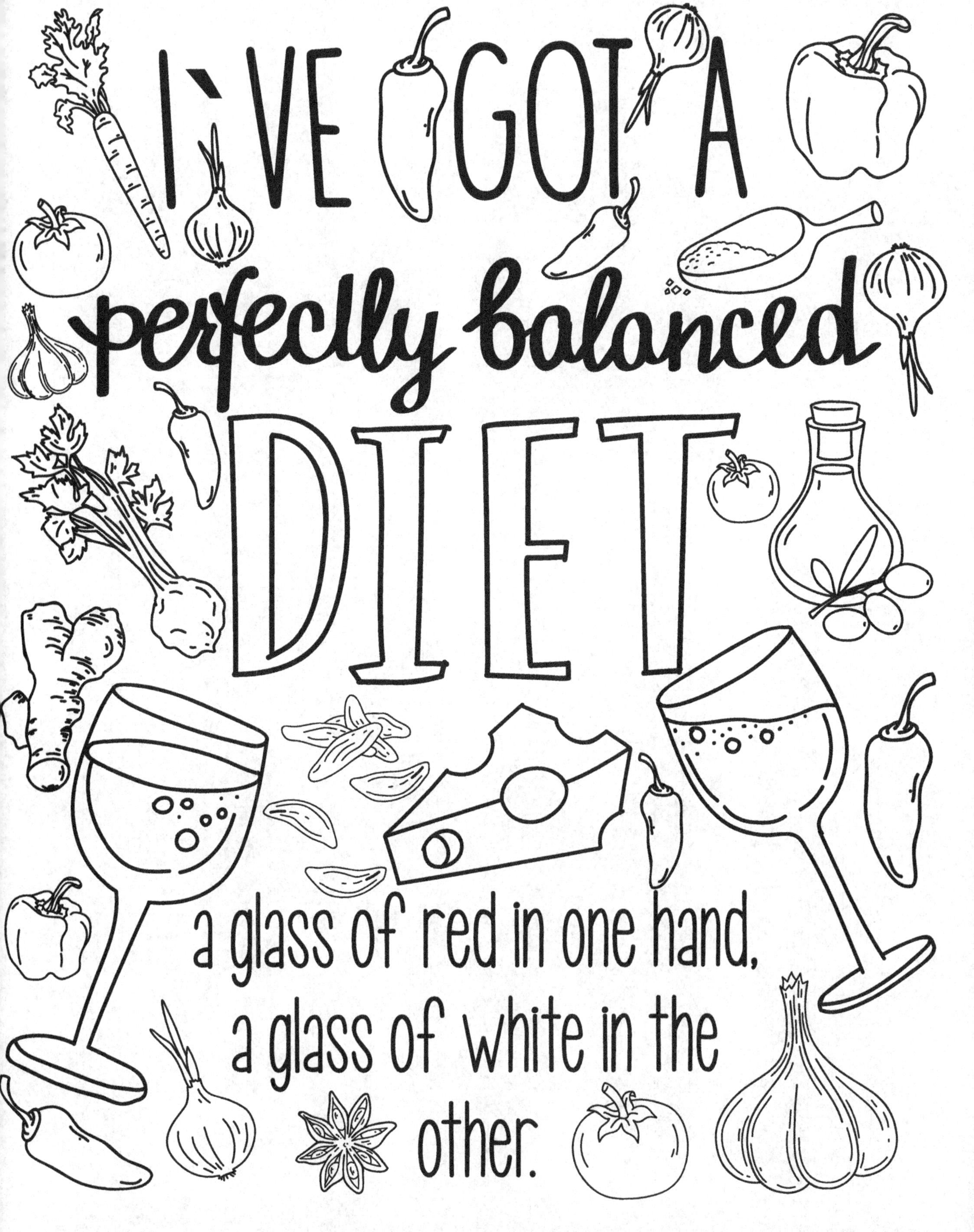
I`VE GOT A
perfectly balanced
DIET
a glass of red in one hand,
a glass of white in the
other.

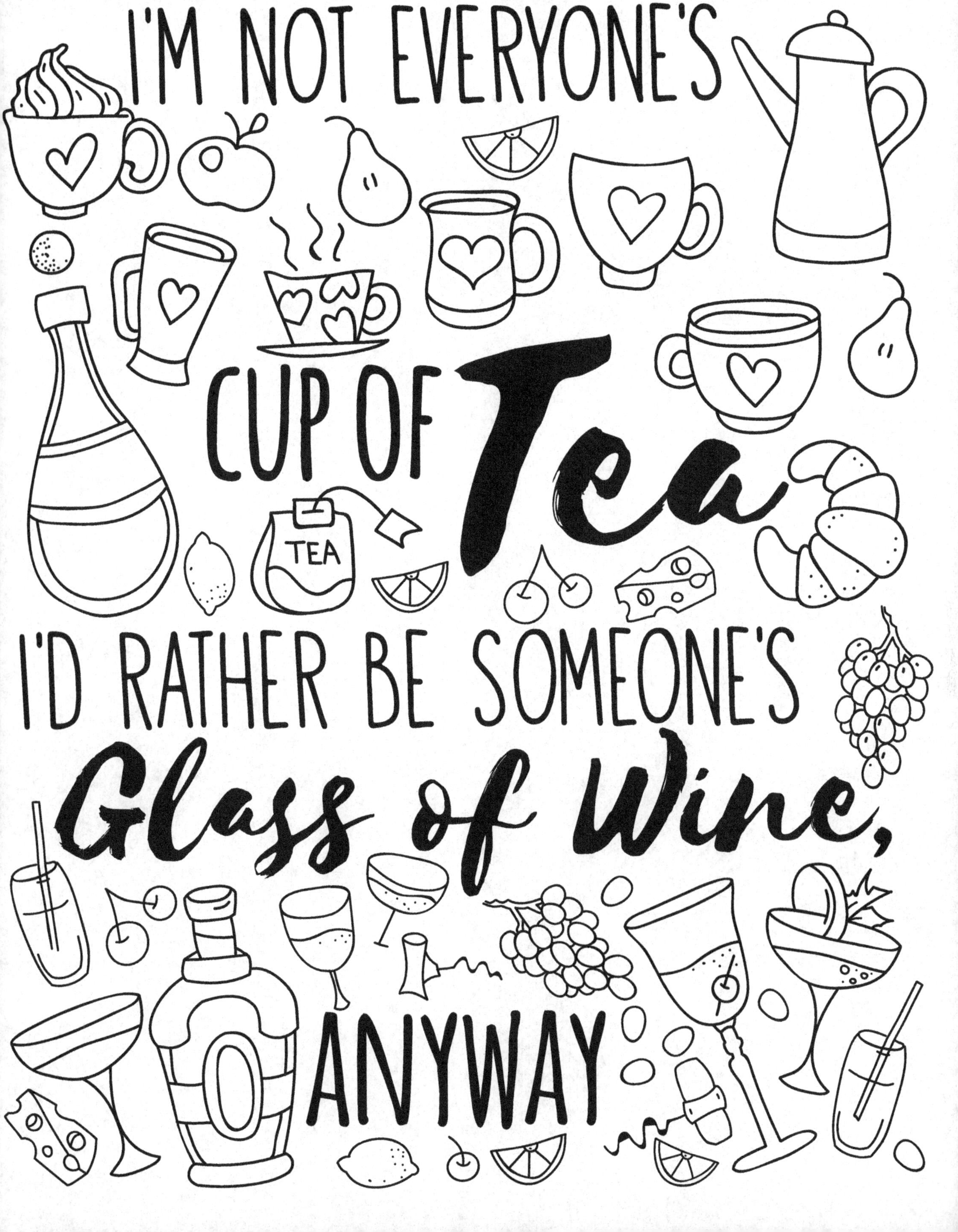
I'M NOT EVERYONE'S
CUP OF Tea
TEA
I'D RATHER BE SOMEONE'S
Glass of Wine,
ANYWAY

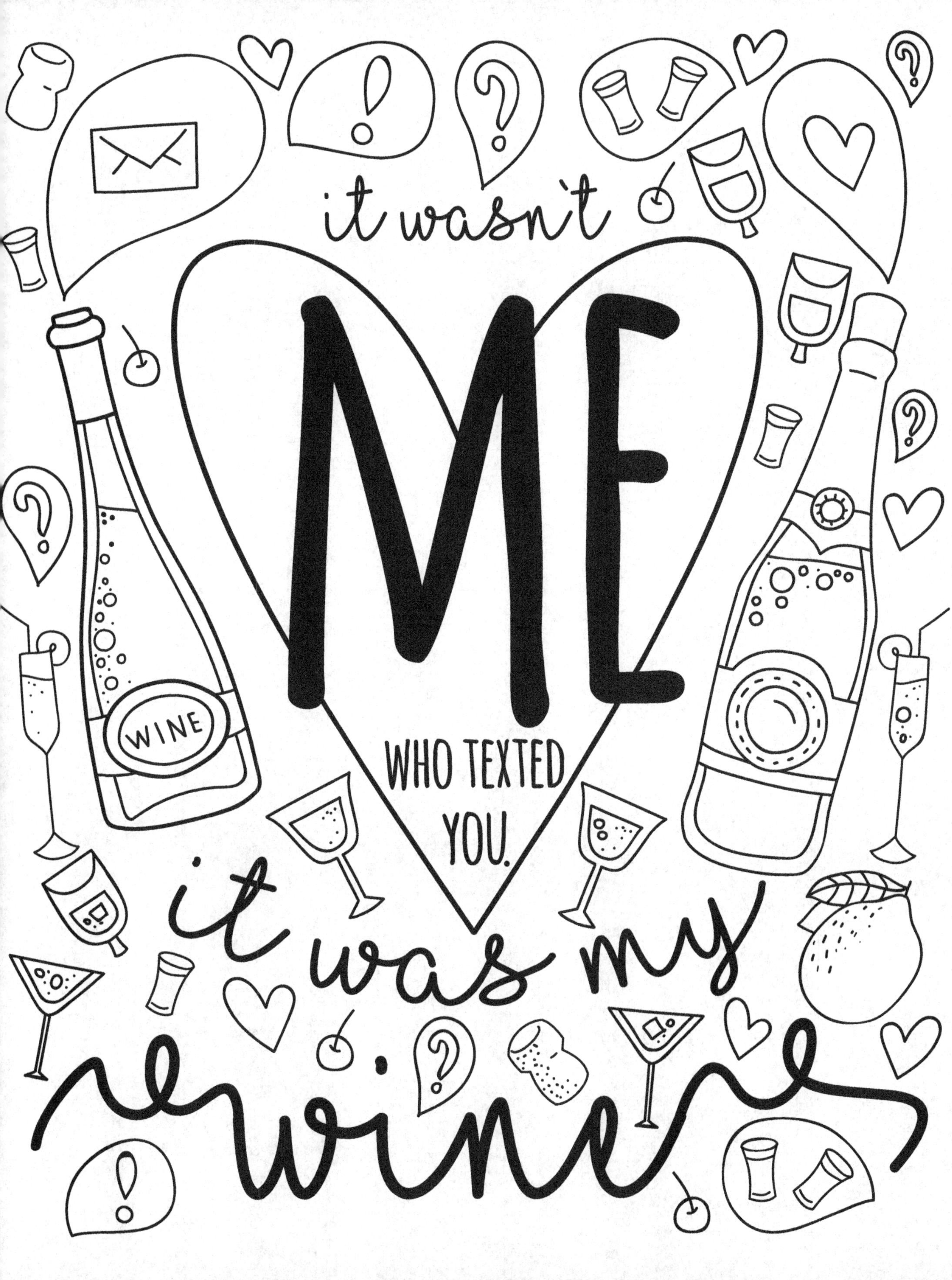
it wasn't
ME
WHO TEXTED YOU.
it was my
wine
WINE

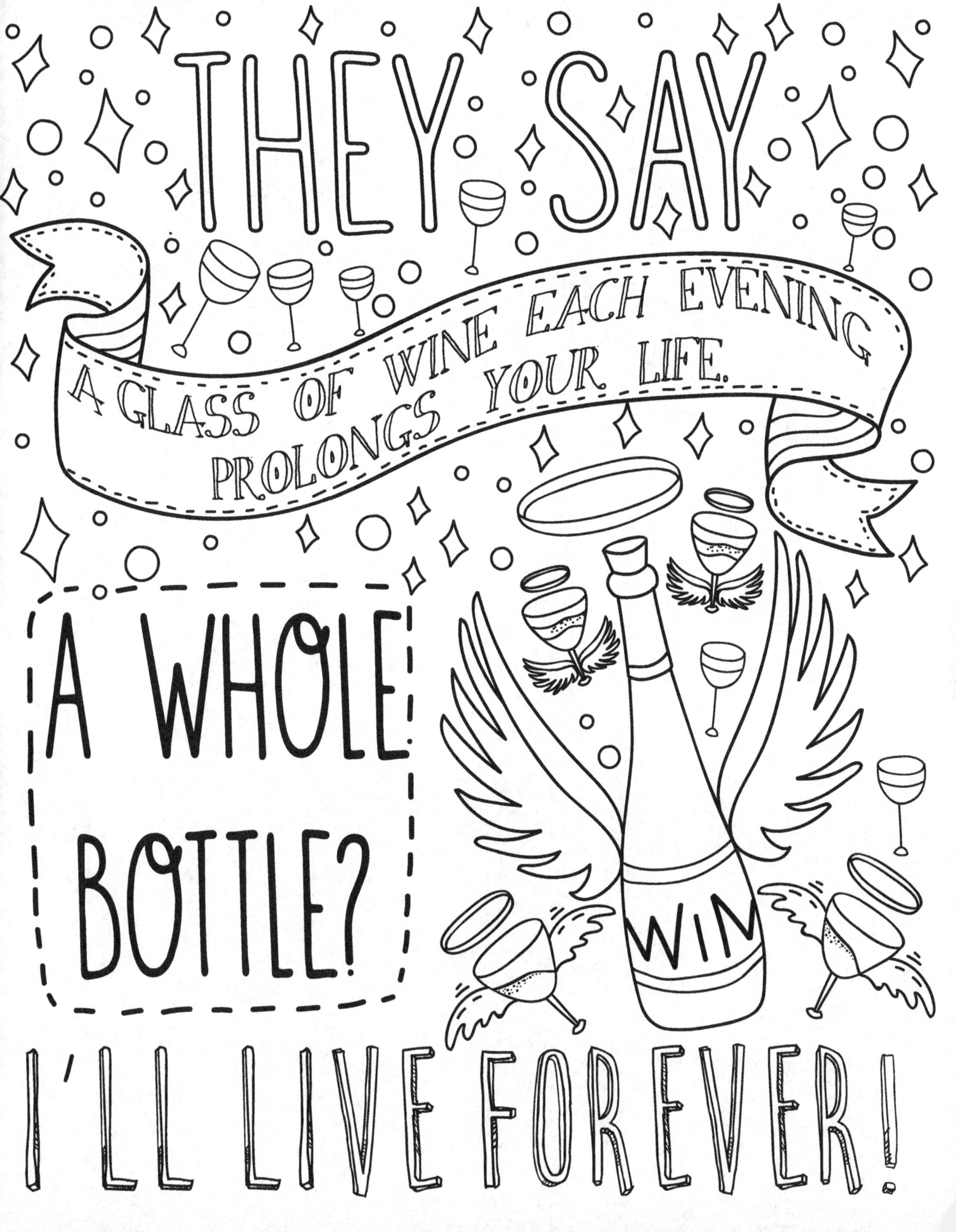
THEY SAY
A GLASS OF WINE EACH EVENING PROLONGS YOUR LIFE.
A WHOLE BOTTLE?
WIN
I'LL LIVE FOREVER!

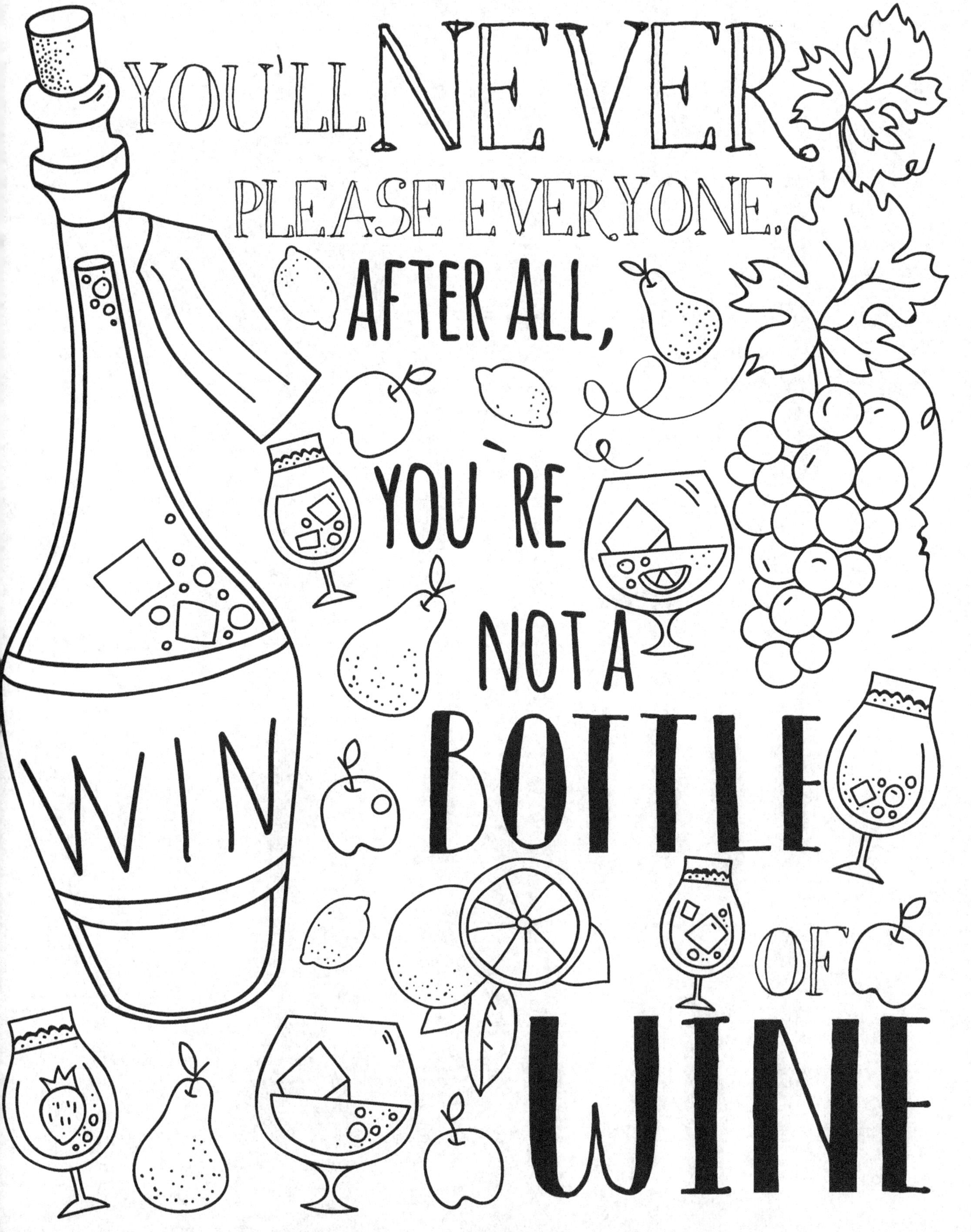
YOU'LL NEVER
PLEASE EVERYONE.
AFTER ALL,
YOU'RE
NOT A
BOTTLE
OF
WINE
WIN

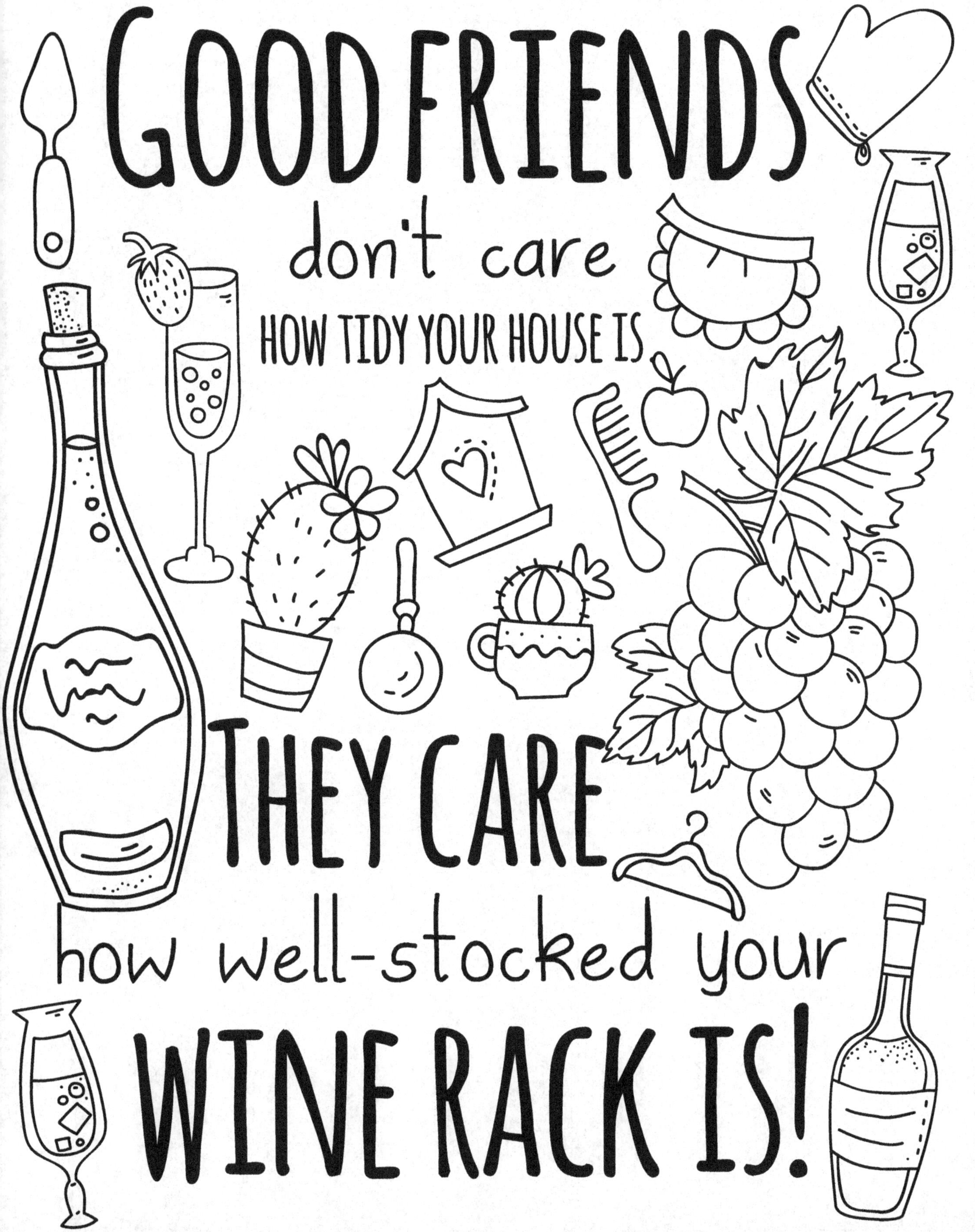
GOOD FRIENDS
don't care
HOW TIDY YOUR HOUSE IS.
THEY CARE
how well-stocked your
WINE RACK IS!

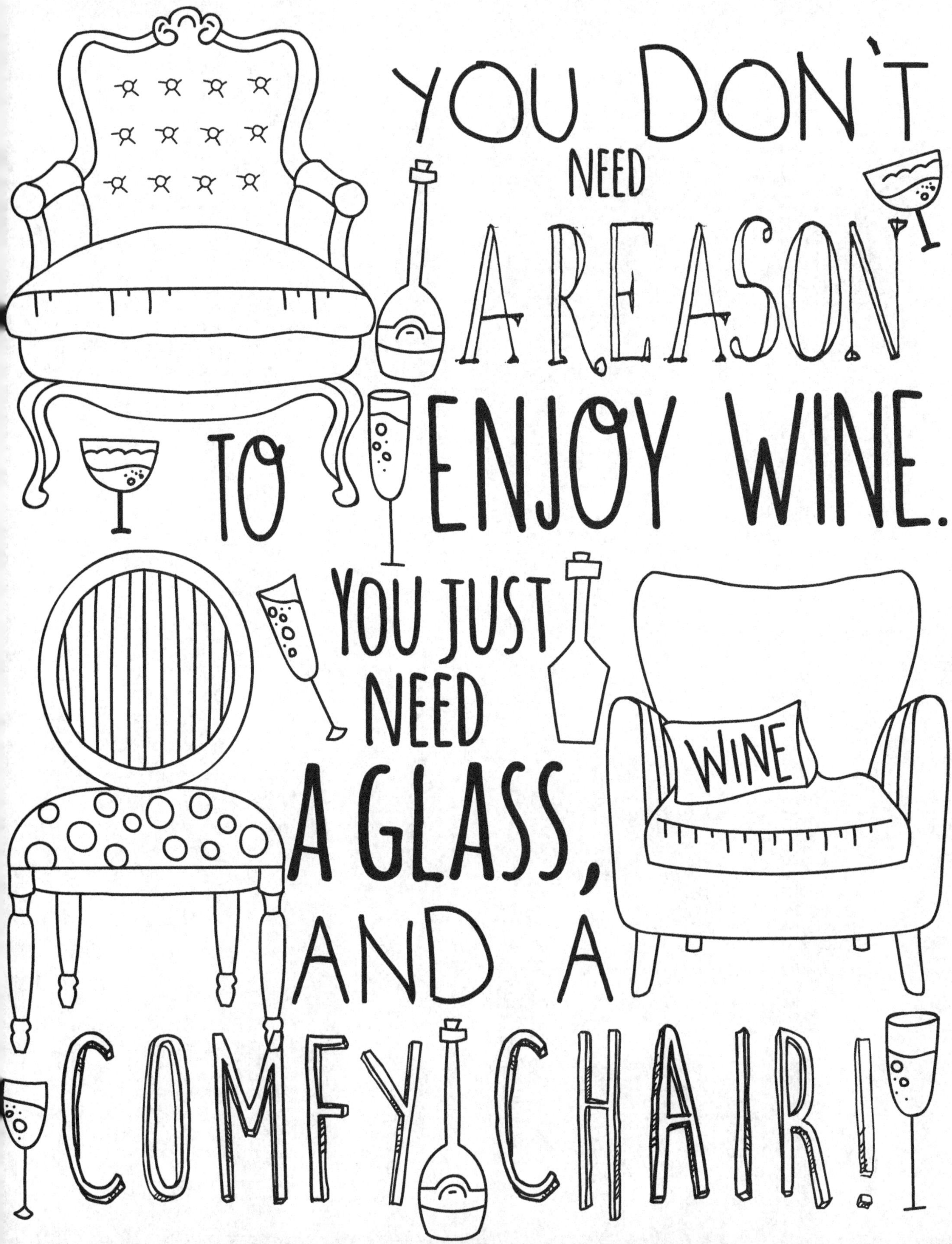
YOU DON'T NEED A REASON TO ENJOY WINE.
YOU JUST NEED A GLASS, AND A COMFY CHAIR!
WINE

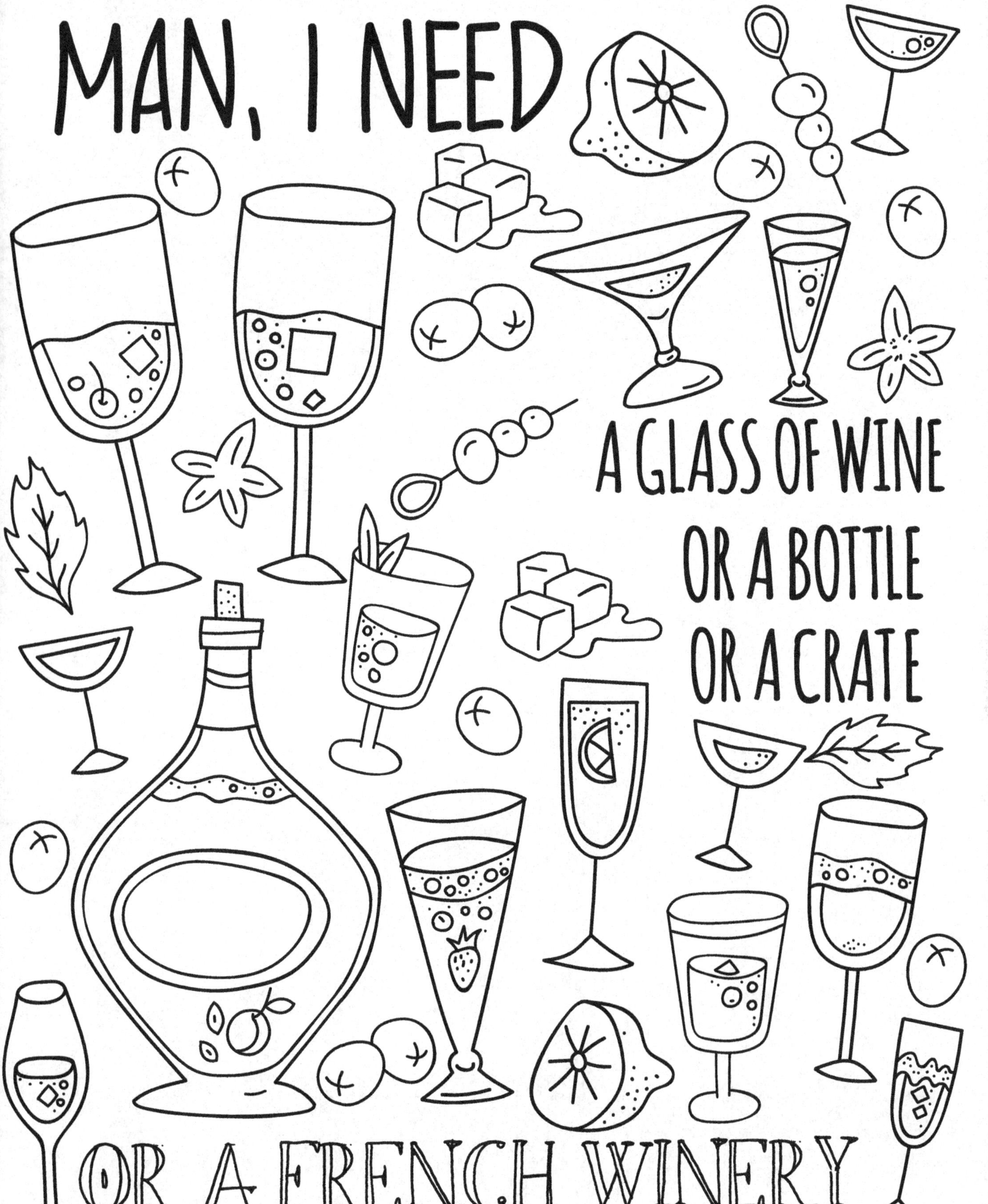
MAN, I NEED
A GLASS OF WINE
OR A BOTTLE
OR A CRATE
OR A FRENCH WINERY

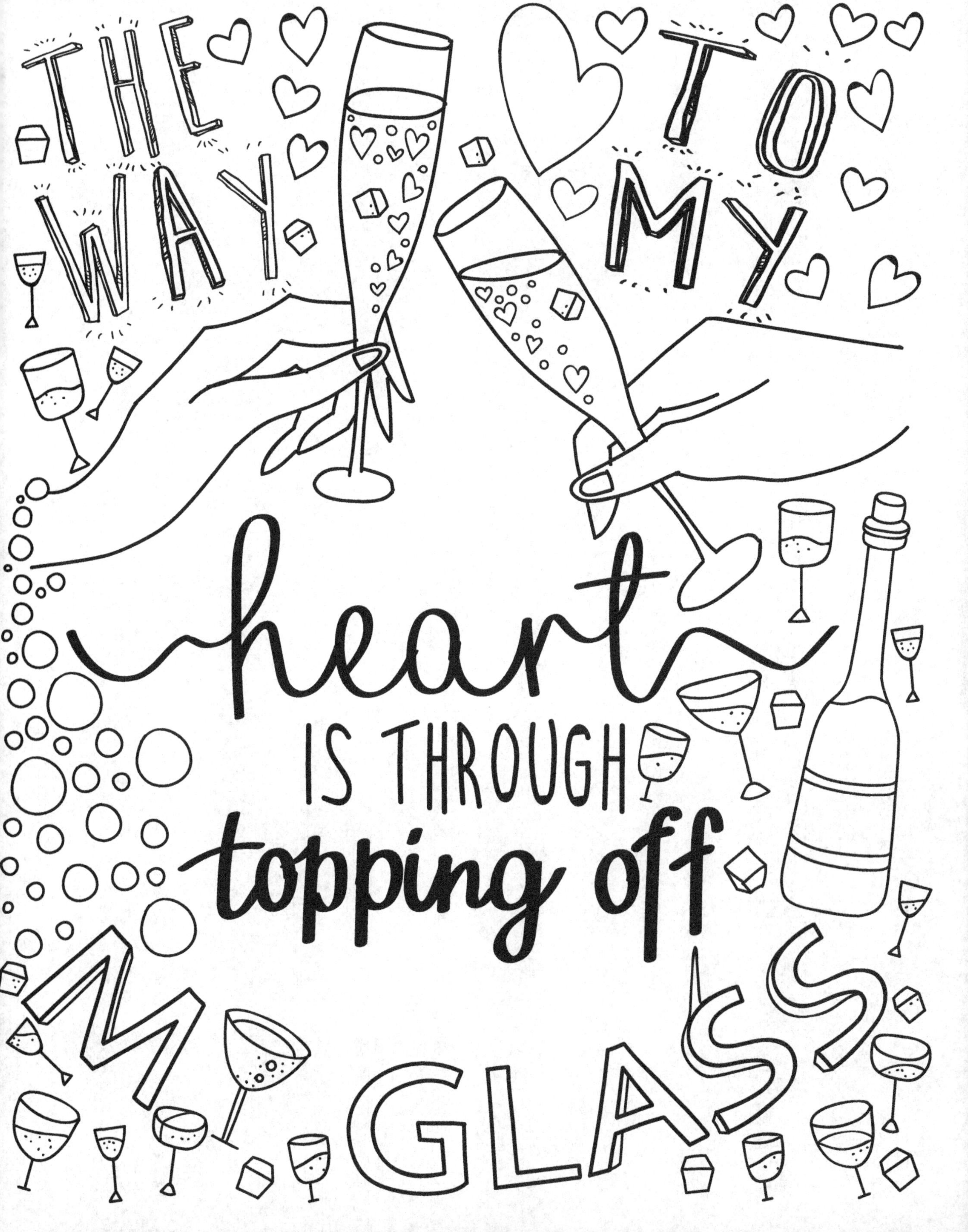
THE WAY TO MY
heart
IS THROUGH
topping off
MY GLASS

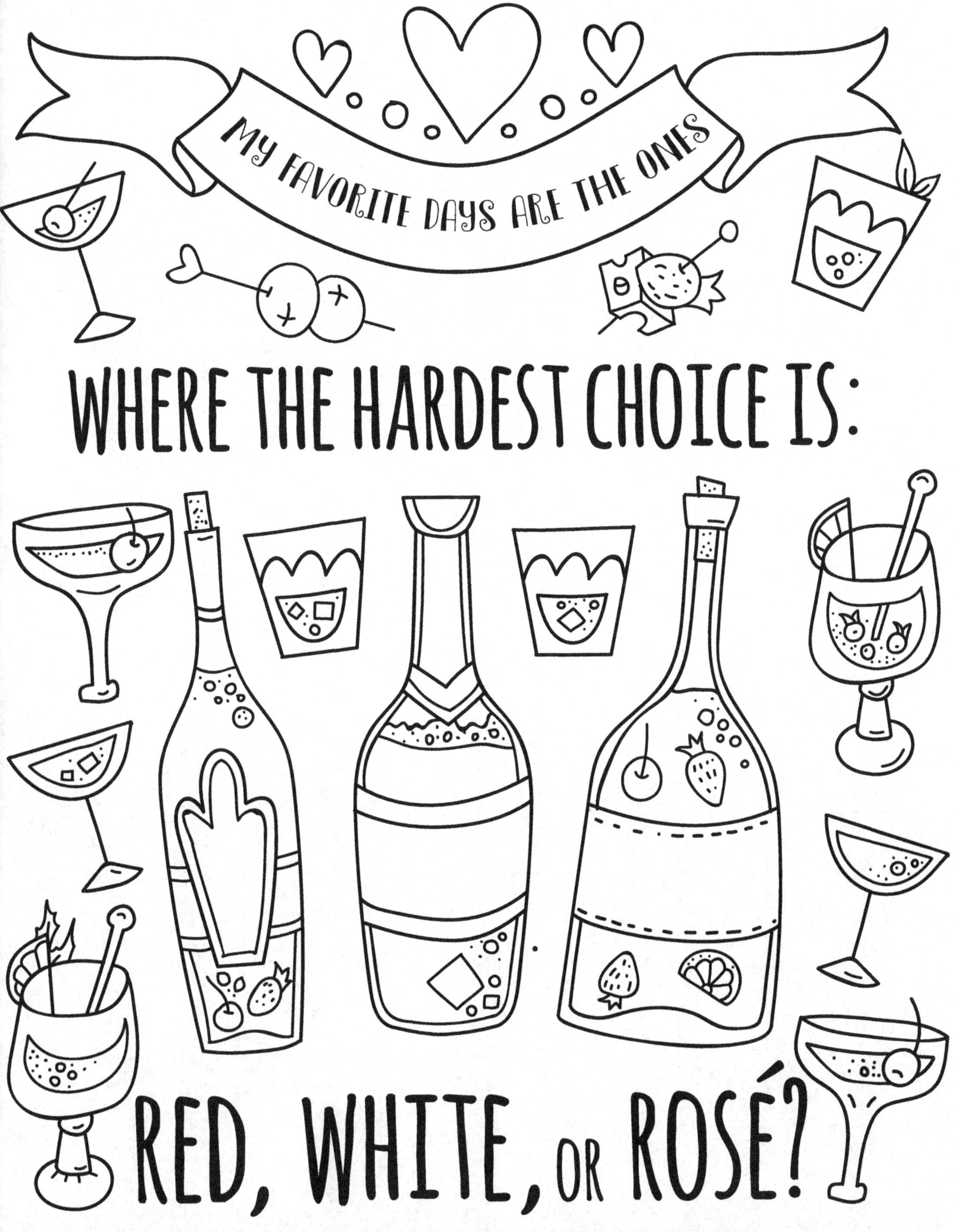
MY FAVORITE DAYS ARE THE ONES
WHERE THE HARDEST CHOICE IS:
RED, WHITE, OR ROSÉ?

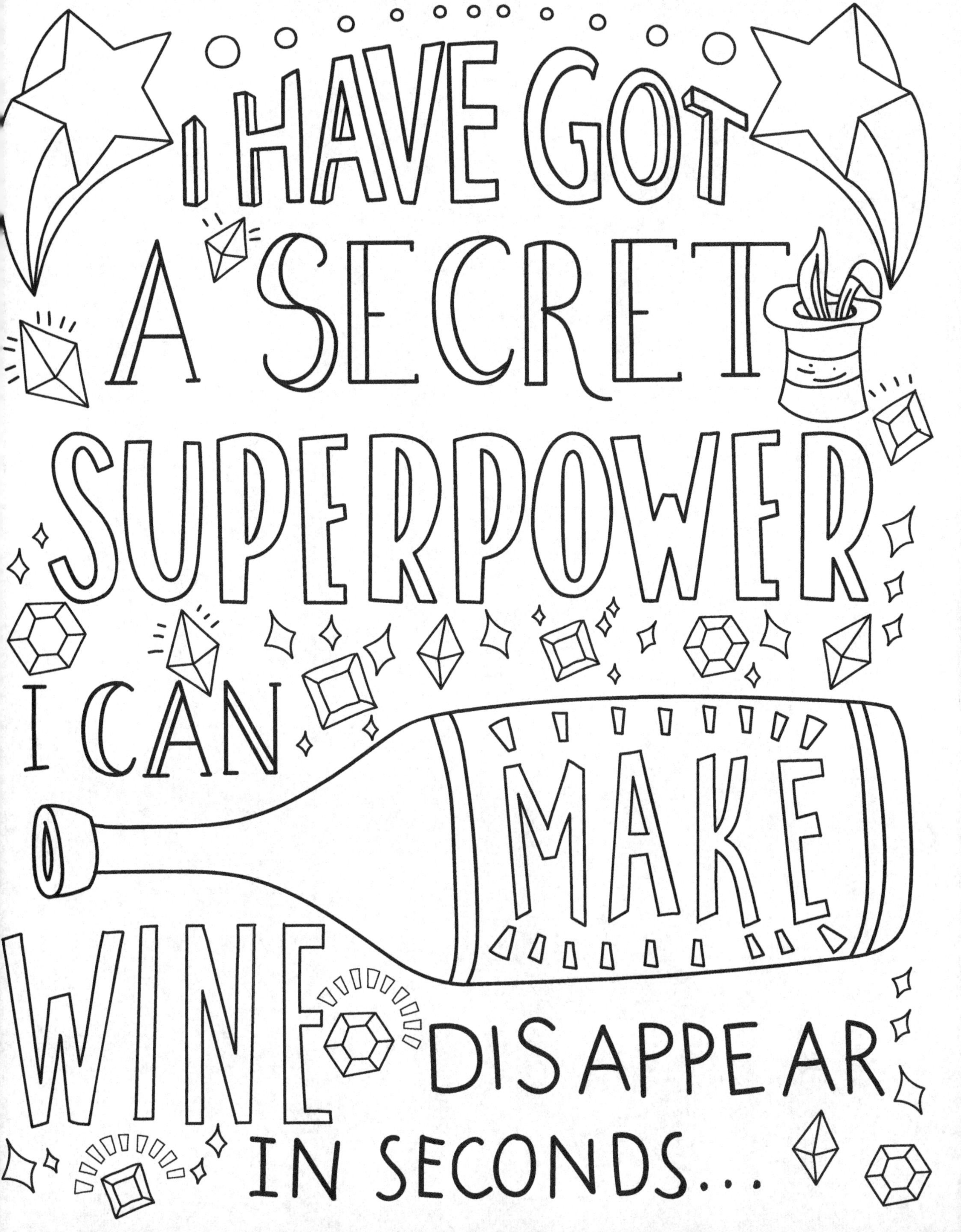
I HAVE GOT
A SECRET
SUPERPOWER
I CAN
MAKE
WINE
DISAPPEAR
IN SECONDS...

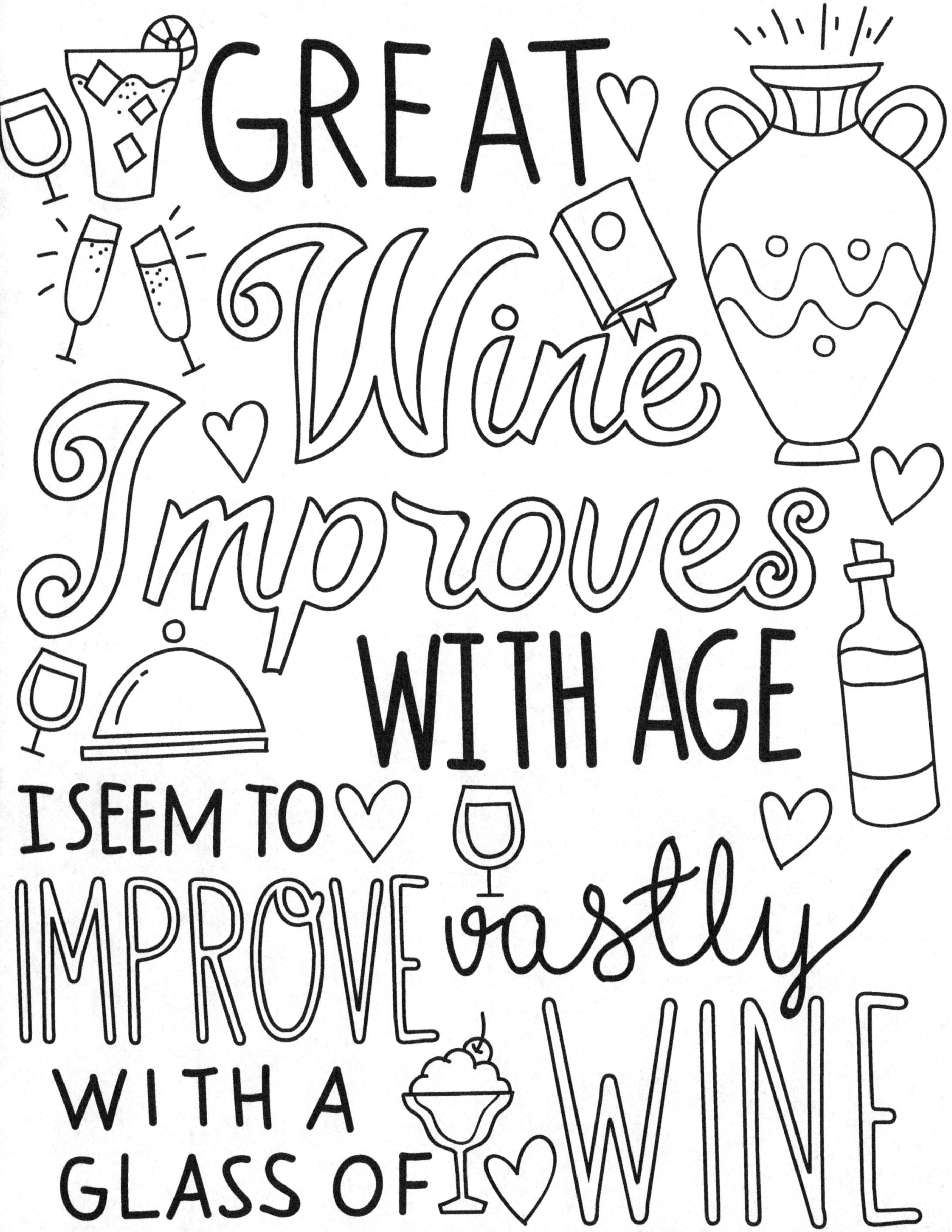
GREAT
Wine
Improves
WITH AGE
I SEEM TO
IMPROVE vastly
WITH A
GLASS OF WINE

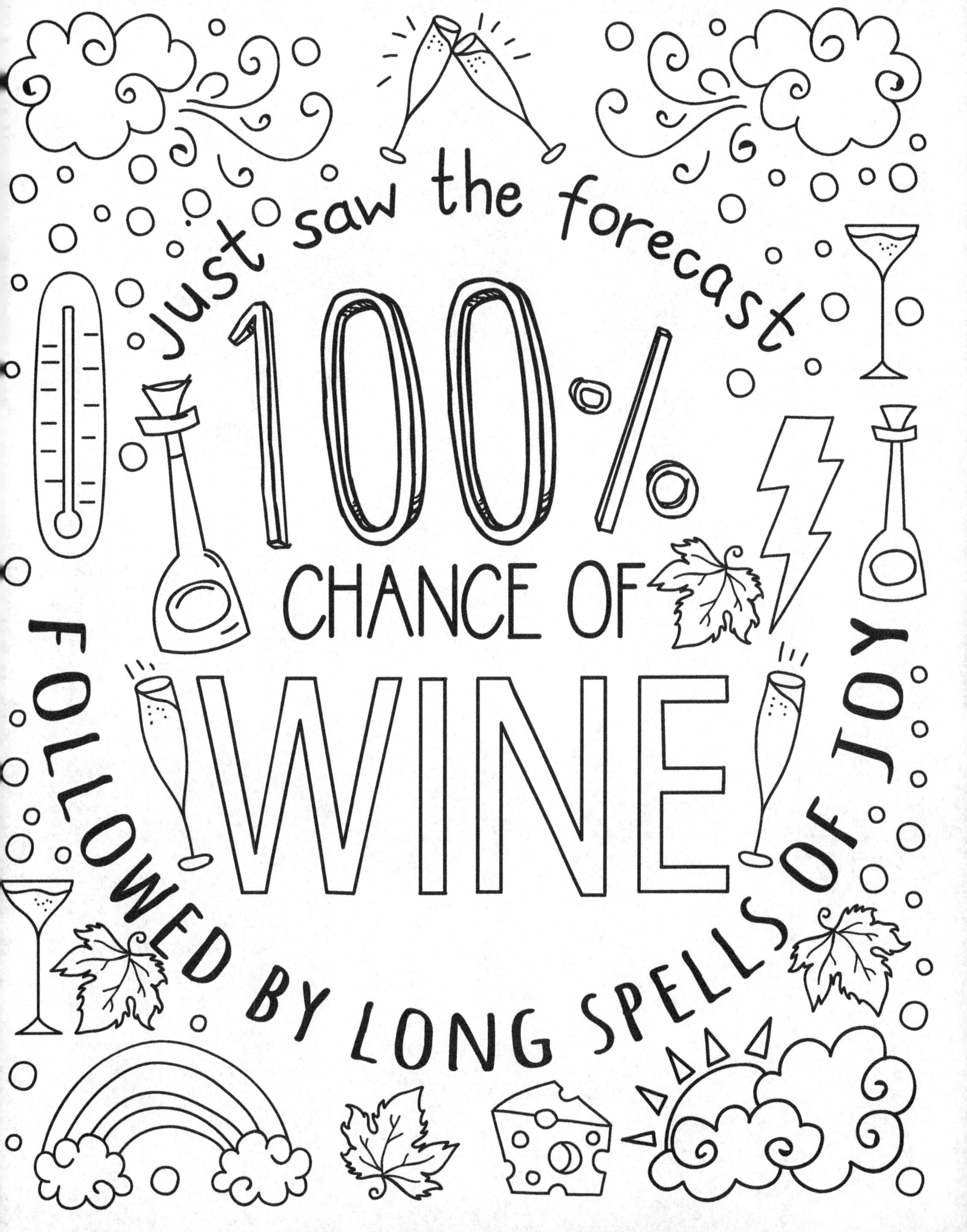
just saw the forecast
100%
CHANCE OF
WINE!
FOLLOWED BY LONG SPELLS OF JOY

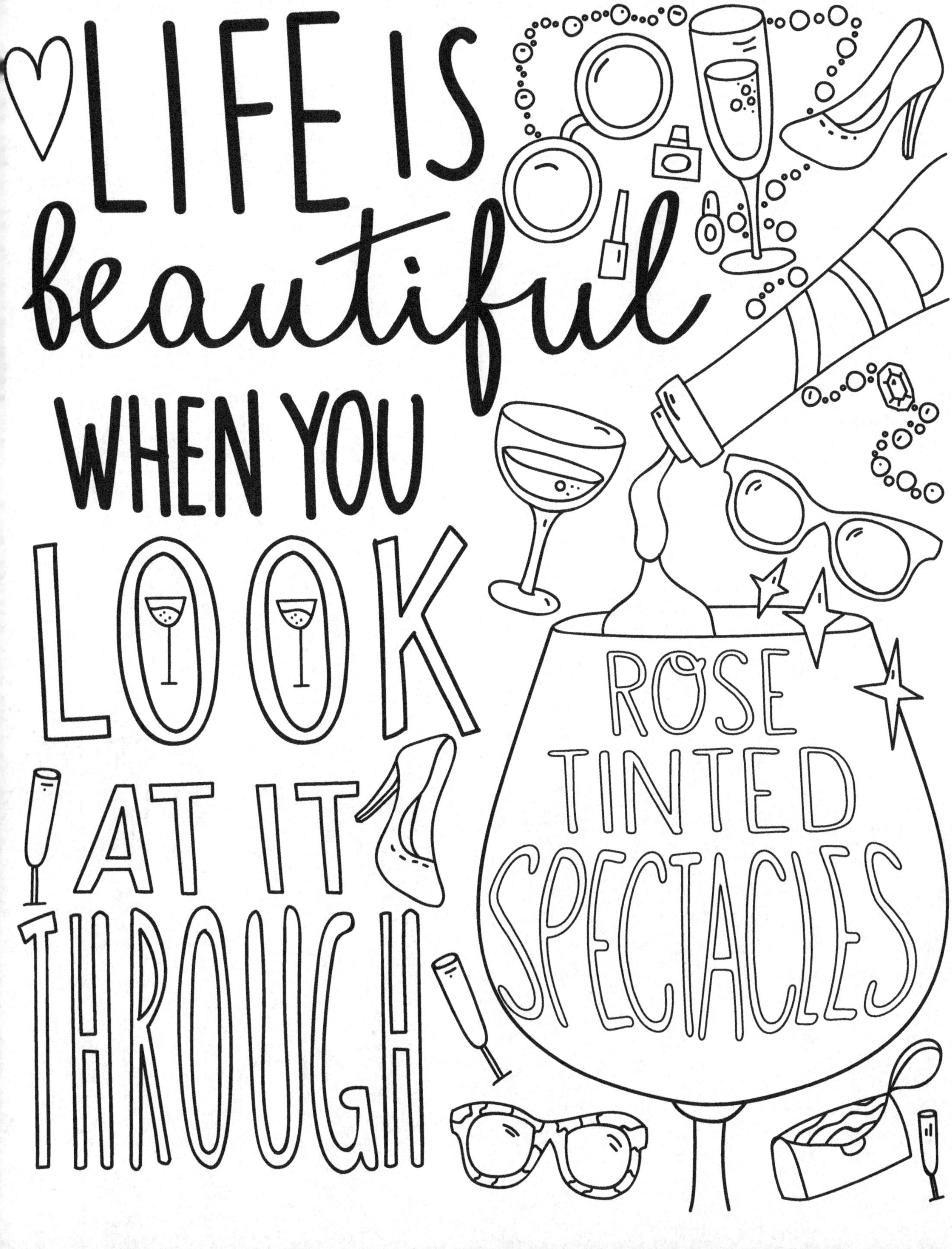
LIFE IS
beautiful
WHEN YOU
LOOK
AT IT
THROUGH
ROSE
TINTED
SPECTACLES

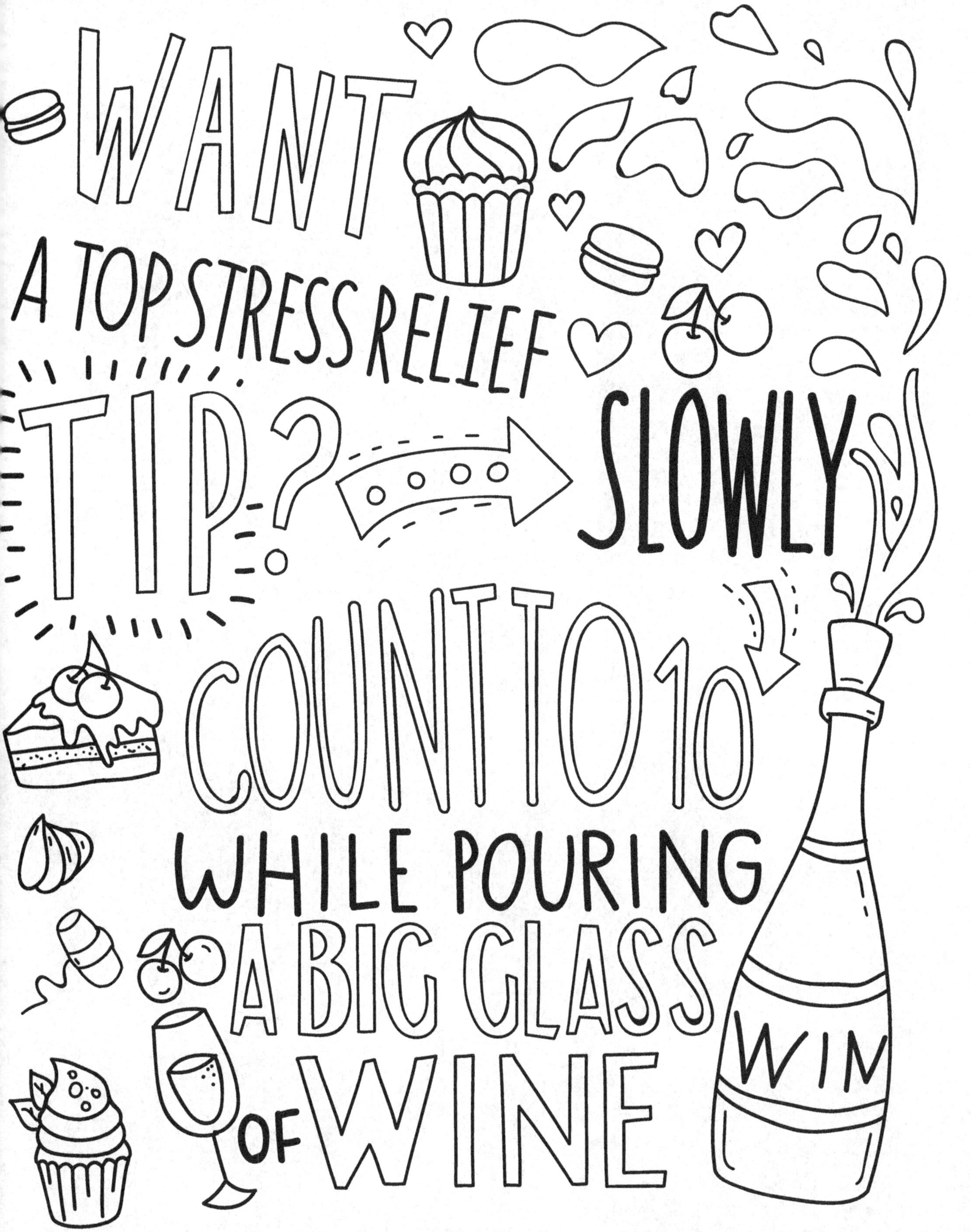
WANT
A TOP STRESS RELIEF
TIP?
SLOWLY
COUNT TO 10
WHILE POURING
A BIG GLASS
OF WINE
WIN

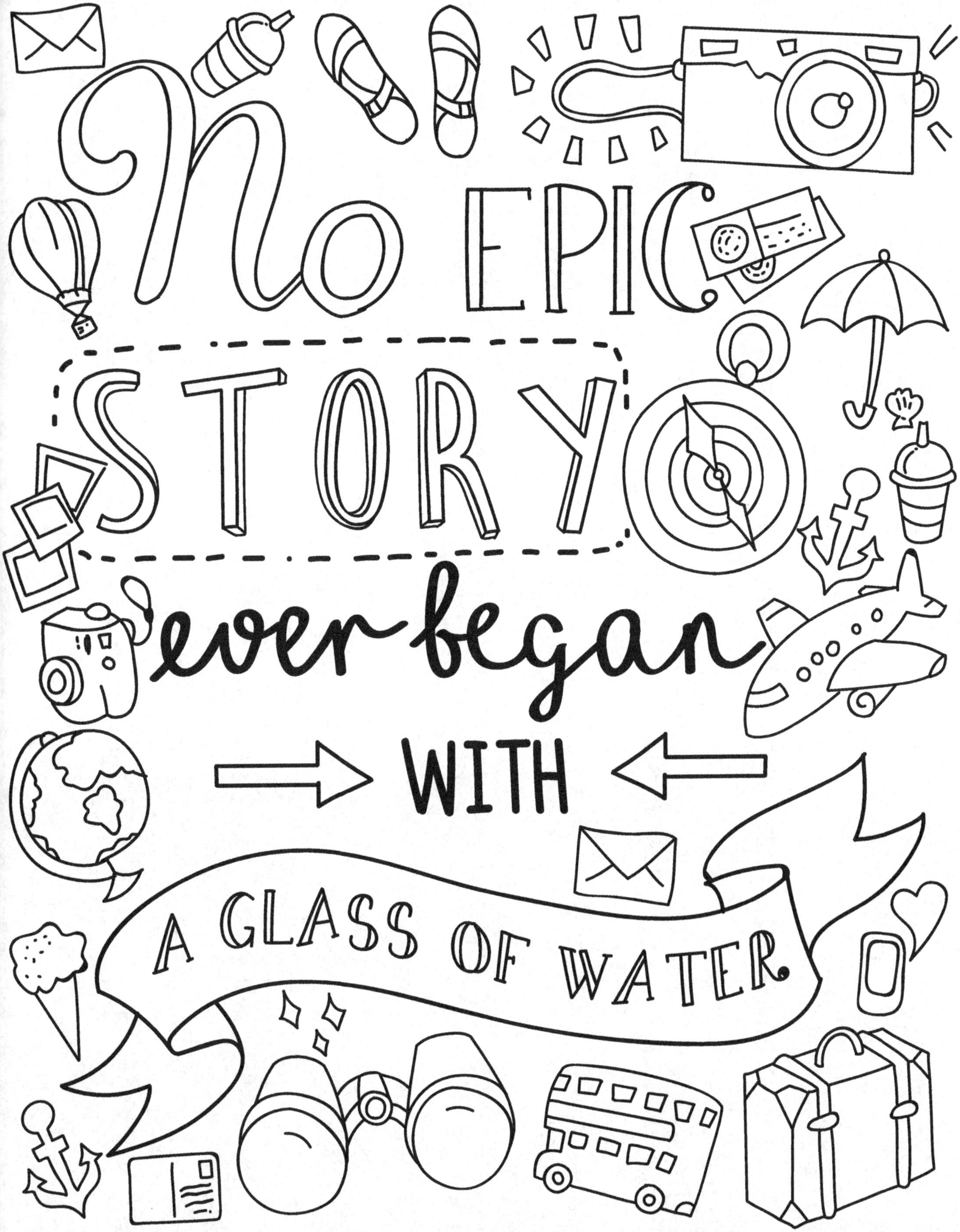
No EPIC
STORY
ever began
WITH
A GLASS OF WATER.

Made in the USA
Coppell, TX
24 October 2021

64615276R00057